Contents

Chapter 1: Introduction to Android Development

Section 1.1: Getting Started with Android

Android is a popular mobile operating system developed by Google. It powers a wide range of devices, including smartphones, tablets, smartwatches, and even televisions. If you're interested in developing applications for the Android platform, you're in the right place. This section will guide you through the initial steps to get started with Android app development.

The Android Ecosystem

Before we dive into the technical details, let's take a moment to understand the Android ecosystem. Android applications are primarily written in Java or Kotlin, two widely used programming languages. These apps run on the Android operating system, which is built on a modified version of the Linux kernel.

Android Studio

To develop Android apps, you'll need a development environment. Google provides Android Studio, a powerful integrated development environment (IDE) designed specifically for Android. Android Studio offers tools, emulators, and a code editor tailored for Android development.

Setting Up Android Studio

Let's begin by setting up Android Studio on your computer. You can download the latest version of Android Studio from the official Android developer website. Once downloaded, follow the installation instructions for your operating system.

Installing the Android SDK

Android Studio relies on the Android Software Development Kit (SDK) to build, test, and run Android apps. During the installation process, Android Studio will guide you through downloading the necessary SDK components. Make sure to install the SDK platforms and system images relevant to the Android versions you intend to target.

Creating Your First Android Project

Now that Android Studio is installed and configured, it's time to create your first Android project. Android projects are organized into apps, each with its own unique functionality. To create an app, open Android Studio and select "Start a new Android Studio project." Follow the wizard, providing the app's name, package name, and other details as prompted.

Understanding the Project Structure

Android Studio creates a project with a predefined structure. The core components of an Android project include:

1. **app/src/main**: This directory contains the main source code and resources for your app.
2. **app/build.gradle**: This file specifies the app's build configuration and dependencies.
3. **app/src/main/AndroidManifest.xml**: The manifest file defines essential information about your app, such as its name, permissions, and entry points.

Running Your First App

With your project created, you can now run your first Android app. Android Studio provides emulators that simulate various Android devices. You can also connect a physical Android device to your computer for testing. To run the app, click the "Run" button in Android Studio's toolbar, and select the target device or emulator.

Congratulations! You've taken your first steps into Android development. In the next sections, we'll explore more aspects of Android app development, including user interfaces, app architecture, and app distribution.

Section 1.2: Overview of Android App Development

In this section, we will provide you with an overview of the Android app development process. Understanding the key concepts and components of Android app development will help you navigate the journey more effectively.

Android App Components

Android apps are built using a variety of components, each with a specific purpose:

1. **Activities**: Activities represent the UI and user interaction of an app. They are individual screens or windows that users can see and interact with.

2. **Fragments**: Fragments are reusable UI components within an activity. They allow you to create flexible and responsive user interfaces.

3. **Services**: Services are background processes that run independently of the UI. They are often used for tasks that should continue running even when the app is not in the foreground.

4. **Broadcast Receivers**: Broadcast receivers listen for system-wide events or broadcasts and respond to them. For example, you can use broadcast receivers to react to changes in network connectivity.

5. **Content Providers**: Content providers manage data and allow it to be shared between different parts of your app or with other apps. They are often used to access databases or content stored on the device.

Understanding the Android app lifecycle is crucial for managing your app's behavior as it transitions between different states:

1. **OnCreate**: This is the first callback method called when an activity or app is created. It is where you typically initialize essential components.

2. **OnStart**: Called when an activity becomes visible to the user, but it is not yet in the foreground.

3. **OnResume**: This method is called when the activity is about to start interacting with the user. It's a good place to start animations or play audio.

4. **OnPause**: Called when the activity is no longer in the foreground, but the user can still see it. You should pause ongoing actions in this method.

5. **OnStop**: Called when the activity is no longer visible to the user. You can release resources here.

6. **OnDestroy**: This method is called when the activity is being destroyed. It's the last callback before the activity is removed from memory.

User Interface (UI) Design

A well-designed user interface is critical for the success of your Android app. Android provides a wide range of UI components, including buttons, text fields, lists, and more. You can design your app's UI using XML layout files or programmatically in code.

Here's a simple example of an XML layout for a button:

```
<Button
    android:id="@+id/myButton"
    android:layout_width="wrap_content"
    android:layout_height="wrap_content"
    android:text="Click Me"
    />
```

Development Languages

Android apps can be developed using Java or Kotlin. Kotlin, a modern programming language, has become increasingly popular for Android development due to its concise syntax and safety features. You can choose the language that best suits your development preferences.

Debugging and Testing

Android Studio provides robust tools for debugging and testing your apps. You can set breakpoints in your code, inspect variables, and use the Android Emulator to simulate different devices and scenarios. Additionally, you can write unit tests to ensure the correctness of your code.

Version Compatibility

Android devices run various versions of the Android operating system. It's essential to consider version compatibility when developing your app. Android provides tools for specifying the minimum and target Android versions your app supports.

Conclusion

This overview has introduced you to the fundamental aspects of Android app development. As you progress through this book, you'll dive deeper into each topic and gain the skills needed to build engaging and functional Android applications. Whether you're creating your first app or expanding your expertise, Android development offers a vast and exciting world of possibilities.

Section 1.3: Setting Up Your Development Environment

Before you start developing Android applications, it's crucial to set up your development environment properly. A well-configured environment ensures a smooth development workflow. In this section, we will walk you through the steps of setting up your development environment for Android.

Android Studio Installation

Android Studio is the official integrated development environment (IDE) for Android app development. To get started, download Android Studio from the official Android developer website (https://developer.android.com/studio). Make sure to download the appropriate version for your operating system (Windows, macOS, or Linux).

Once the download is complete, follow the installation instructions for your platform. Android Studio will guide you through the installation process, including the installation of necessary SDK components.

Android SDK and API Levels

The Android Software Development Kit (SDK) contains the libraries and tools needed for Android app development. Android Studio installs the SDK components automatically during setup. However, you can also install additional SDK packages as needed, especially if you plan to target specific Android versions.

When developing an Android app, you'll need to specify the minimum and target Android API levels. The minimum API level determines the lowest version of Android your app can run on, while the target API level specifies the version you are primarily developing for.

You can configure these settings in your app's `build.gradle` file, as shown below:

```
android {
    compileSdkVersion 31
    defaultConfig {
```

```
        applicationId "com.example.myapp"
        minSdkVersion 21
        targetSdkVersion 31
        // ...
    }
    // ...
}
```

Android Emulator or Physical Device

To test your Android applications, you have two primary options: using the Android Emulator or a physical Android device. Android Studio includes a built-in emulator that allows you to simulate various Android devices and configurations.

To create a virtual device in the emulator, go to the "AVD Manager" in Android Studio. You can choose from a variety of device profiles, each emulating different screen sizes, resolutions, and hardware features.

If you prefer testing on a physical device, you can connect your Android device to your development computer via USB. Ensure that USB debugging is enabled on your device in the Developer Options settings.

Developer Options and USB Debugging

On your Android device, you'll need to enable Developer Options and USB debugging to deploy and test apps directly from Android Studio.

To enable Developer Options: 1. Open the "Settings" app on your Android device. 2. Scroll down and select "About Phone." 3. Find the "Build Number" entry and tap it repeatedly (usually seven times) until you see a message indicating that Developer Options have been enabled.

To enable USB debugging: 1. In the Developer Options, enable the "USB debugging" option.

Now, when you connect your Android device to your computer via USB, you can deploy and run apps on it from Android Studio.

Creating Your First Project

With Android Studio installed and your development environment set up, you're ready to create your first Android project. Android Studio provides templates for various app types, making it easy to start with a basic project structure. You can create a new project by selecting "Start a new Android Studio project" from the welcome screen.

Follow the project creation wizard, where you'll set the project name, package name, and select the target Android version. Android Studio will generate the initial project files and structure for you.

In summary, setting up your development environment involves installing Android Studio, configuring the Android SDK and API levels, setting up emulators or connecting physical devices, enabling Developer Options and USB debugging on your Android device, and creating your first Android project. With these steps completed, you're ready to embark on your Android app development journey.

Section 1.4: Creating Your First Android Project

Now that you've set up your development environment, it's time to create your first Android project. In this section, we'll walk you through the process of creating a basic Android project using Android Studio.

Launch Android Studio

Start by launching Android Studio on your computer. If you've just installed it, you can find Android Studio in your applications or program list. Upon opening Android Studio, you'll be greeted with the welcome screen.

Start a New Android Project

To create a new Android project, follow these steps:

1. Click on "Start a new Android Studio project" on the welcome screen.

2. The "Create New Project" wizard will appear. You'll need to provide some essential project details:

    - **Name**: Enter a name for your project. This is how your project will be identified within Android Studio.

    - **Package name**: This is a unique identifier for your app. Typically, it follows the reverse domain name convention (e.g., `com.example.myapp`).

    - **Save location**: Choose where you want to save your project files on your computer.

    - **Language**: Select either Java or Kotlin as your programming language. Kotlin is the recommended language for modern Android development due to its concise syntax and safety features.

    - **Minimum API level**: Choose the minimum Android version your app will support. This determines the oldest devices your app can run on.

    - **Template**: You can choose from various templates, such as "Empty Activity" or "Basic Activity," to start with a pre-configured project structure.

3. After filling in the project details, click the "Finish" button to create your project.

Exploring the Project Structure

Android Studio will generate the initial project structure for you. Let's take a quick look at some of the essential files and folders:

- **app/src/main**: This directory contains your app's source code, including activities, fragments, and other Java or Kotlin classes.

- **app/src/main/res**: This folder stores your app's resources, such as layout XML files, drawables, and string resources.

- **app/src/main/AndroidManifest.xml**: This XML file defines essential information about your app, such as permissions, activities, and services.

- **app/build.gradle**: This file specifies your app's build configuration, dependencies, and version information.

Designing Your App's User Interface

One of the first things you'll want to do in your Android project is to design the user interface (UI) of your app. Android provides two primary methods for creating UI layouts: XML layout files and programmatically in code.

To design your UI using XML, you can create or modify XML layout files in the res/layout directory. Here's a simple example of an XML layout for a button:

```
<Button
    android:id="@+id/myButton"
    android:layout_width="wrap_content"
    android:layout_height="wrap_content"
    android:text="Click Me"
    />
```

You can also use Android's drag-and-drop UI designer to create layouts visually.

Running Your App

With your project set up and your UI designed, it's time to run your app. You can do this by clicking the "Run" button (a green triangle) in the Android Studio toolbar. You can choose to run your app on an emulator or a connected physical device.

The first run may take a little longer as Android Studio builds and deploys your app. Once the app is running, you'll see it on the emulator or your device, and you can interact with it.

Conclusion

Creating your first Android project is an exciting step in your Android development journey. In this section, you've learned how to start a new project, explore the project structure, design your app's UI, and run your app for testing. As you progress further, you'll dive deeper into app development concepts and build more sophisticated Android applications.

Section 1.5: Emulators and Physical Devices for Testing

When developing Android applications, it's essential to have a reliable method for testing your apps. In this section, we'll explore two primary options for testing your Android apps: using emulators and testing on physical Android devices.

Android Emulators

Android Studio provides a built-in emulator that allows you to simulate various Android devices and configurations. Emulators are valuable tools for testing your apps on different screen sizes, resolutions, and Android versions without the need for physical devices.

Setting Up an Emulator

To set up an emulator in Android Studio, follow these steps:

1. Open Android Studio.

2. Click on "Tools" in the top menu and select "AVD Manager."

3. In the AVD Manager, click the "Create Virtual Device" button.

4. Choose a hardware profile for your emulator. You can select from a list of predefined profiles or create a custom one.

5. Select a system image for the Android version you want to simulate. If you haven't downloaded the required system image yet, click the "Download" link next to it.

6. Configure additional options such as RAM size, device orientation, and more.

7. Click "Finish" to create the emulator.

Running Your App on an Emulator

Once you've set up an emulator, you can run your app on it:

1. Make sure the emulator is running and fully loaded.

2. In Android Studio, click the "Run" button (the green triangle) in the toolbar.

3. Select your emulator as the deployment target.

4. Android Studio will build your app and deploy it to the emulator.

5. You'll see your app running on the emulator, and you can interact with it as if it were a physical device.

Physical Android Devices

While emulators are useful for testing, it's also crucial to test your app on real Android devices, as they can provide a more accurate representation of user experiences. Here's how you can set up and test on physical Android devices:

Enabling Developer Options and USB Debugging

Before you can test on a physical device, you need to enable Developer Options and USB debugging on the device. Here are the steps:

1. On your Android device, go to "Settings."

2. Scroll down and select "About Phone."

3. Find the "Build Number" entry and tap it repeatedly (usually seven times) until you see a message indicating that Developer Options have been enabled.

4. In the Developer Options, enable the "USB debugging" option.

Connecting Your Device

Connect your Android device to your computer using a USB cable. Make sure that USB debugging is enabled on your device, as mentioned in the previous step.

Running Your App on a Physical Device

To run your app on a physical Android device:

1. In Android Studio, click the "Run" button in the toolbar.

2. Select your connected device as the deployment target.

3. Android Studio will build your app and deploy it to the connected device.

4. You'll see your app running on the physical device, and you can interact with it.

Testing on Multiple Devices

It's essential to test your app on multiple physical devices to ensure compatibility and a consistent user experience. Different devices may have varying screen sizes, resolutions, and hardware capabilities.

Conclusion

In this section, you've learned about two primary methods for testing your Android apps: using emulators and testing on physical Android devices. Emulators are useful for simulating different device configurations, while testing on real devices provides a more authentic experience. Depending on your project's requirements, you may use both emulators and physical devices to ensure your app works well across a range of platforms.

Chapter 2: Android Fundamentals

Section 2.1: The Android Architecture

Understanding the Android architecture is essential for any Android developer. Android operates on a layered architecture, with each layer serving a specific purpose in the app's execution. In this section, we will delve into the core components of the Android architecture.

Linux Kernel

At the base of the Android architecture is the Linux kernel. Android is built on top of a modified Linux kernel, which provides essential hardware abstraction and management services. The Linux kernel is responsible for tasks such as memory management, process management, and hardware driver interaction.

Libraries and Android Runtime

Above the Linux kernel, you find a set of libraries and the Android Runtime (ART). These components form the foundation for the Android platform:

- **Libraries**: Android includes a wide range of libraries for various purposes. These libraries provide functionalities for tasks like graphics rendering, database access, web browsing, and more. For example, the OpenGL ES library is used for 3D graphics rendering, while SQLite provides database management.

- **Android Runtime (ART)**: ART is the runtime environment for Android apps. It executes compiled code using a technique called Ahead-of-Time (AOT) compilation, which improves app performance. In earlier Android versions, the Dalvik virtual machine was used, but ART has become the standard.

Core Libraries

Android's core libraries include:

- **java.lang**: This package provides fundamental classes and exceptions that are part of the Java standard library.

- **java.util**: It contains utility classes for working with collections, data structures, and other common tasks.

- **android.app**: This package contains the core components of Android apps, such as Activity, Service, and BroadcastReceiver.

- **android.content**: It offers classes for content providers, which allow apps to share data and access data from other apps.

The Application Framework layer provides high-level building blocks for Android app development. It includes the following components:

- **Activities**: Activities are the user interface components of Android apps. They represent individual screens or windows where user interactions occur.

- **Services**: Services are background processes that perform long-running operations without a user interface. They are used for tasks like playing music, syncing data, or handling network requests.

- **Content Providers**: Content providers manage and share structured data, such as databases or files, between apps. They facilitate data sharing while maintaining security and data isolation.

- **Broadcast Receivers**: Broadcast receivers listen for system-wide events or custom broadcasts and respond to them. They are often used for tasks like reacting to incoming SMS messages or network connectivity changes.

Above the Application Framework layer, you have two categories of apps:

- **System Apps**: These are pre-installed apps that come with the Android operating system. Examples include the Phone app, Messaging app, and Settings app.

- **User Apps**: These are the apps installed by users from the Google Play Store or other sources. User apps can be developed by third-party developers.

The Android architecture consists of multiple layers, each serving a specific purpose in the execution of Android apps. Understanding this architecture is crucial for building efficient and effective Android applications. In the following sections, we will explore various components of the Android architecture in more detail, including Activities, Intents, Views, and more.

Section 2.2: Activities and User Interfaces

In the Android architecture, Activities play a central role in defining the user interface and user interaction of an app. Activities represent individual screens or windows that users can see and interact with. In this section, we will explore Activities in more detail and discuss how they are used to create user interfaces.

Understanding Activities

An Activity in Android is a Java or Kotlin class that extends the `android.app.Activity` class. Each Activity corresponds to a single screen in your app, and it defines the user interface and interaction for that screen. For example, you might have one Activity for displaying a login screen and another for showing a user's profile.

Here's a basic example of an Activity in Kotlin:

```kotlin
import android.app.Activity
import android.os.Bundle

class LoginActivity : Activity() {
    override fun onCreate(savedInstanceState: Bundle?) {
        super.onCreate(savedInstanceState)
        setContentView(R.layout.activity_login)
        // Other initialization code goes here
    }
}
```

In the example above, `LoginActivity` is an Activity that is responsible for displaying the login screen. The `onCreate` method is called when the Activity is created, and it typically sets the layout of the screen using `setContentView`. The layout is defined in an XML file, such as `activity_login.xml`.

Activity Lifecycle

Activities have a lifecycle that defines their state and the sequence of method calls. Understanding the Activity lifecycle is crucial for managing the behavior of your app as it transitions between different states. The primary lifecycle methods include:

- `onCreate`: Called when the Activity is first created. This is where you typically perform one-time initialization, such as setting up the UI.

- `onStart`: Called when the Activity becomes visible to the user, but it's not yet in the foreground. You can start animations or initiate loading data here.

- `onResume`: Called when the Activity is about to start interacting with the user. This is a good place to start audio playback or initiate location updates.

- `onPause`: Called when the Activity is no longer in the foreground but is still visible. You should pause ongoing actions here.

- `onStop`: Called when the Activity is no longer visible to the user. You can release resources here.

- `onDestroy`: Called when the Activity is being destroyed. It's the last callback before the Activity is removed from memory.

You can override these methods in your Activity class to perform specific actions at each stage of the lifecycle.

Activities are responsible for defining the user interface (UI) of your app. You can create the UI using XML layout files, which describe the layout and appearance of the screen. Here's a simplified example of an XML layout for a login screen:

```xml
<?xml version="1.0" encoding="utf-8"?>
<LinearLayout xmlns:android="http://schemas.android.com/apk/res/android"
    android:layout_width="match_parent"
    android:layout_height="match_parent"
    android:orientation="vertical">

    <EditText
        android:id="@+id/editTextUsername"
        android:layout_width="match_parent"
        android:layout_height="wrap_content"
        android:hint="Username" />

    <EditText
        android:id="@+id/editTextPassword"
        android:layout_width="match_parent"
        android:layout_height="wrap_content"
        android:hint="Password"
        android:inputType="textPassword" />

    <Button
        android:id="@+id/buttonLogin"
        android:layout_width="match_parent"
        android:layout_height="wrap_content"
        android:text="Login" />
</LinearLayout>
```

This XML layout defines a simple login screen with two EditText fields for the username and password and a login Button.

Starting Activities

In Android, you can start a new Activity by creating an Intent and calling startActivity. An Intent is an object that describes an operation to be performed, such as starting a new Activity. Here's an example of how to start a new Activity:

```kotlin
val intent = Intent(this, LoginActivity::class.java)
startActivity(intent)
```

In this example, we create an Intent to start the LoginActivity, and then we call startActivity to initiate the transition to that Activity.

Conclusion

Activities are a fundamental part of Android app development, responsible for defining user interfaces and user interactions. Understanding the Activity lifecycle and how to create and start Activities is essential for building effective Android applications. In the next sections, we will explore more aspects of Android app development, including Intents, Views, and Layouts.

Section 2.3: Intents and Navigation

In Android, navigation between different screens (Activities) and the communication between components are achieved using Intents. Intents are a fundamental concept in Android app development, allowing you to trigger various actions, such as starting a new Activity, broadcasting events, or opening system services. In this section, we'll explore Intents and their role in navigating between screens.

What Is an Intent?

An Intent is an object that represents an abstract description of an operation to be performed. It acts as a message between components in an Android app or between different Android apps. Intents are used to trigger actions or requests, and they can carry data.

There are two primary types of Intents in Android:

1. **Explicit Intents**: These Intents specify the exact component (Activity, Service, or BroadcastReceiver) to be invoked. They are typically used for internal navigation within your app.

2. **Implicit Intents**: Implicit Intents do not specify a particular component; instead, they describe the desired action, and Android's system selects an appropriate component to fulfill the request. Implicit Intents are often used for actions that can be performed by multiple apps, such as sharing content.

Creating and Using Intents

To create and use Intents in your Android app, you need to follow a few key steps:

Creating an Intent

You create an Intent by specifying the action you want to perform and, optionally, the data you want to send. Here's an example of creating an explicit Intent to navigate from one Activity to another:

```
val intent = Intent(this, SecondActivity::class.java)
```

In this example, SecondActivity::class.java specifies the target Activity we want to navigate to.

Starting an Activity with an Intent

To start a new Activity using an Intent, you use the `startActivity(intent)` method. For example:

```
startActivity(intent)
```

This code snippet will start the `SecondActivity` from the current Activity.

Passing Data with Intents

Intents can also carry data between components. You can use methods like `putExtra()` to attach data to an Intent and `getXXXExtra()` methods to retrieve it. For example, to pass a string to another Activity:

```kotlin
val intent = Intent(this, SecondActivity::class.java)
intent.putExtra("message", "Hello from the first Activity!")
startActivity(intent)
```

In the receiving Activity (in this case, `SecondActivity`), you can retrieve the data like this:

```kotlin
val message = intent.getStringExtra("message")
```

Implicit Intents

Implicit Intents are used to request actions from other apps or system components. For example, to open a web page:

```kotlin
val intent = Intent(Intent.ACTION_VIEW, Uri.parse("https://www.example.com"))
startActivity(intent)
```

In this case, we create an implicit Intent with the action `ACTION_VIEW` to open a web page specified by the URI.

Intent Filters

To respond to implicit Intents, components in your app can declare Intent Filters in the AndroidManifest.xml file. An Intent Filter specifies the types of Intents that a component can handle based on actions, categories, and data types.

For example, if you want your Activity to handle incoming share Intents, you can define an Intent Filter like this:

```xml
<activity android:name=".MyActivity">
    <intent-filter>
        <action android:name="android.intent.action.SEND" />
        <category android:name="android.intent.category.DEFAULT" />
        <data android:mimeType="text/plain" />
    </intent-filter>
</activity>
```

Conclusion

Intents are a crucial concept in Android app development, enabling navigation between screens and communication between components. Whether you're using explicit Intents for internal navigation or implicit Intents to interact with other apps, understanding how to create, use, and handle Intents is essential for building feature-rich Android applications. In the following sections, we will explore more topics related to Android app development, including Views, Layouts, and User Interface design principles.

Section 2.4: Views and Layouts

Views and layouts are fundamental components of Android app user interfaces. Views represent UI elements, such as buttons, text fields, and images, while layouts define how these views are organized and displayed on the screen. In this section, we'll explore the concepts of views, layouts, and how they work together to create the user interface of an Android app.

Views

In Android, a View is a basic building block for constructing the user interface. Views represent individual UI elements that users can interact with, such as buttons, text fields, labels, and images. Every visible element on the screen is essentially a View.

Here are some commonly used Views in Android:

- **TextView**: Used for displaying text to the user.
- **EditText**: Allows users to input text.
- **Button**: Represents clickable buttons.
- **ImageView**: Displays images.
- **CheckBox**: Represents a checkbox that users can toggle on or off.
- **RadioButton**: A radio button that allows users to select one option from a list.
- **Spinner**: A drop-down selection list.
- **SeekBar**: A slider for selecting values within a range.

Layouts

While Views represent individual UI elements, Layouts are containers that define how these Views are organized and positioned on the screen. Layouts determine the overall structure and arrangement of Views within an Activity or Fragment.

Some common types of Layouts in Android include:

- **LinearLayout**: Arranges child Views in a linear, horizontal, or vertical fashion. It's straightforward for creating simple layouts.

- **RelativeLayout**: Allows you to position Views relative to each other or to the parent layout. It offers more complex arrangement options.

- **ConstraintLayout**: A powerful and flexible layout that allows you to create complex UIs with responsive designs. It uses constraints to define the position and size of Views.

- **FrameLayout**: Places child Views on top of each other, allowing for layering. It's useful for creating overlays or simple container layouts.

- **GridLayout**: Arranges child Views in a grid-like fashion, where each View occupies a specific grid cell.

XML Layout Files

In Android app development, Views and Layouts are often defined using XML layout files. These files specify the structure and attributes of the user interface elements. XML layout files are stored in the res/layout directory of your project.

Here's a simple example of an XML layout that contains a TextView and a Button arranged in a LinearLayout:

```
<LinearLayout
    xmlns:android="http://schemas.android.com/apk/res/android"
    android:layout_width="match_parent"
    android:layout_height="match_parent"
    android:orientation="vertical">

    <TextView
        android:id="@+id/textView"
        android:layout_width="wrap_content"
        android:layout_height="wrap_content"
        android:text="Hello, Android!" />

    <Button
        android:id="@+id/button"
        android:layout_width="wrap_content"
        android:layout_height="wrap_content"
        android:text="Click Me" />
</LinearLayout>
```

In this example, we define a LinearLayout as the root layout, which contains a TextView and a Button. Each View has its unique ID and attributes, such as width, height, and text.

You can also manipulate Views programmatically using Java or Kotlin code. For example, you can change the text of a TextView, set an OnClickListener for a Button, or dynamically create and add Views to a layout container.

Here's an example of changing the text of a TextView programmatically in Kotlin:

```kotlin
val textView = findViewById<TextView>(R.id.textView)
textView.text = "Updated Text"
```

Combining Views and Layouts

In practice, Android UIs are often built by combining various Views and Layouts. Complex screens may use nested Layouts to achieve the desired structure, with each Layout containing multiple Views. Effective UI design involves selecting the appropriate Views and Layouts to create a user-friendly and visually appealing interface.

Conclusion

Views and Layouts are essential components of Android app user interfaces. Views represent individual UI elements, while Layouts define the arrangement and structure of these Views on the screen. By creating XML layout files and programmatically manipulating Views, you can design interactive and visually appealing user interfaces for your Android apps. In the next section, we will explore user interface design principles specific to Android app development.

Section 2.5: User Interface Design Principles

Effective user interface (UI) design is crucial for creating user-friendly and visually appealing Android apps. In this section, we'll explore some fundamental user interface design principles specific to Android app development.

Material Design

Material Design is a design language introduced by Google, and it's widely adopted in Android app development. It provides a set of guidelines and principles for creating intuitive and visually pleasing user interfaces. Key aspects of Material Design include:

- **Material Surfaces**: Use layers, elevation, and shadows to create a sense of depth in your UI. Elements should appear as if they exist on separate sheets of material.

- **Typography**: Choose appropriate fonts, styles, and sizes for text to ensure readability and hierarchy. Material Design provides guidance on font choices.

- **Color**: Use a color palette that adheres to Material Design guidelines. Colors should have meaning and consistency within your app. Differentiate UI elements with color.

- **Layout and Spacing**: Maintain consistent spacing, alignment, and grid layouts. Use appropriate margins and padding to enhance readability.

- **Motion**: Employ meaningful animations and transitions to guide user interactions. Animations should feel natural and responsive.

Responsive Design

Android apps run on a wide range of devices with varying screen sizes and resolutions. It's essential to create responsive UIs that adapt to different screen sizes and orientations. Android's ConstraintLayout is a powerful tool for building responsive layouts, as it allows you to define flexible constraints between UI elements.

Consistency

Consistency is key to a good user experience. Maintain consistency in the placement of common UI elements like navigation bars, buttons, and menus. Use consistent color schemes, typography, and icons throughout your app. This makes your app more intuitive for users.

Accessibility

Consider accessibility from the beginning of your app design. Ensure that your app is usable by people with disabilities, such as those who rely on screen readers. Provide text descriptions for images, use semantic markup, and follow accessibility guidelines.

User Feedback

Provide clear and timely feedback to users when they perform actions in your app. Use feedback mechanisms like toast messages, progress bars, or animations to indicate that an action has been received and is in progress.

User Testing

Conduct user testing with real users to gather feedback on your app's usability and design. User testing can uncover issues that you may not have noticed and help you make informed design decisions.

Performance

A well-designed UI is responsive and performs well. Optimize your UI for smooth interactions and quick load times. Minimize unnecessary animations and avoid complex layouts that might slow down your app.

User-Centered Design

Always design your app with the end-user in mind. Consider the needs, preferences, and behaviors of your target audience. Conduct user research to gain insights into user expectations and pain points.

Iterative Design

UI design is an iterative process. Don't be afraid to make changes and refinements based on user feedback and testing results. Continuously improve your app's UI to provide the best possible user experience.

Conclusion

User interface design is a critical aspect of Android app development. By following design principles like Material Design, focusing on responsiveness, consistency, accessibility, and user-centered design, you can create Android apps that are not only visually appealing but also user-friendly and enjoyable to use. Keep in mind that UI design is an ongoing process of refinement, and user feedback is invaluable for making your app even better.

Chapter 3: Building Your First Android App

Section 3.1: Creating a Simple User Interface

Creating a user interface (UI) is one of the fundamental steps in building an Android app. The UI defines how users interact with your app and how information is presented to them. In this section, we'll walk through the process of creating a simple user interface for your Android app.

XML Layout Files

Android uses XML (Extensible Markup Language) files to define the layout and structure of your app's user interface. These XML layout files are located in the res/layout directory of your Android project. Android Studio provides a visual editor that makes it easy to create and modify these XML files, but you can also edit them directly in text form.

Here's a basic example of an XML layout file that defines a simple user interface with a TextView and a Button:

```xml
<?xml version="1.0" encoding="utf-8"?>
<LinearLayout
    xmlns:android="http://schemas.android.com/apk/res/android"
    android:layout_width="match_parent"
    android:layout_height="match_parent"
    android:orientation="vertical">

    <TextView
        android:id="@+id/textView"
        android:layout_width="wrap_content"
        android:layout_height="wrap_content"
        android:text="Hello, Android!"
        android:textSize="24sp" />

    <Button
        android:id="@+id/button"
        android:layout_width="wrap_content"
        android:layout_height="wrap_content"
        android:text="Click Me" />
</LinearLayout>
```

In this XML layout, we use a LinearLayout as the root layout container. Inside the LinearLayout, we have a TextView with the text "Hello, Android!" and a Button with the label "Click Me."

Layout Attributes

Each UI element in your XML layout file has a set of attributes that control its appearance and behavior. In the example above, we set attributes such as `android:id`, `android:layout_width`, `android:layout_height`, `android:text`, and `android:textSize`.

- `android:id`: An identifier for the View, which allows you to reference it in your code.

- `android:layout_width` and `android:layout_height`: Specify the width and height of the View. Common values include `wrap_content` and `match_parent`.

- `android:text`: Sets the text displayed by a TextView or Button.

- `android:textSize`: Defines the text size in scaled pixels (sp).

Previewing Your Layout

Android Studio provides a visual layout editor that allows you to preview your XML layout files. You can switch between the code and design views to make adjustments. The design view provides a WYSIWYG (What You See Is What You Get) interface for designing your UI.

Referencing Views in Code

To interact with UI elements in your code, you need to reference them by their IDs. In the XML layout example, we gave the TextView an ID of "textView" and the Button an ID of "button." Here's how you can reference these Views in your code:

```
val textView = findViewById<TextView>(R.id.textView)
val button = findViewById<Button>(R.id.button)
```

Once you have references to your Views, you can programmatically modify their properties or respond to user interactions, such as button clicks.

Running Your App

To see your UI in action, you need to run your app on an emulator or a physical device. Android Studio provides tools for building and deploying your app to various targets. Click the "Run" button in Android Studio to build and run your app.

Conclusion

Creating a simple user interface is the first step in building an Android app. XML layout files define the structure and appearance of your UI elements, and you can reference these elements in your code to add functionality. Android Studio's visual editor makes it easy to design your UI, and running your app on an emulator or device allows you to see it in action. In the next sections, we will explore handling user interaction, adding functionality, and testing your app.

Section 3.2: Handling User Interaction

Handling user interaction is a fundamental part of building Android apps. User interfaces are designed for users to interact with your app, and it's essential to capture and respond to their actions effectively. In this section, we'll explore various ways to handle user interaction in your Android app.

User Interface Elements

Before diving into handling user interaction, it's crucial to understand the user interface elements you'll be working with. Android provides a wide range of UI elements, including buttons, text fields, checkboxes, radio buttons, and more. Each element serves a specific purpose and can trigger user actions.

OnClickListener

One of the most common ways to handle user interaction is by using the OnClickListener interface. It allows you to listen for clicks on UI elements like buttons and respond to them with specific actions.

Here's an example of setting an OnClickListener for a Button in Kotlin:

```kotlin
val button = findViewById<Button>(R.id.button)
button.setOnClickListener {
    // Handle button click here
}
```

You can define the desired behavior inside the lambda function, and it will execute when the button is clicked.

Handling Text Input

When working with text input fields, such as EditText, you can capture user input by registering an event listener. For instance, if you want to respond to text changes in an EditText field, you can use a TextWatcher:

```kotlin
val editText = findViewById<EditText>(R.id.editText)
editText.addTextChangedListener(object : TextWatcher {
    override fun beforeTextChanged(s: CharSequence?, start: Int, count: Int,
after: Int) {
        // Called before text changes
    }

    override fun onTextChanged(s: CharSequence?, start: Int, before: Int, cou
nt: Int) {
        // Called during text changes
    }
```

```kotlin
    override fun afterTextChanged(s: Editable?) {
        // Called after text changes
    }
})
```

This allows you to perform actions based on text input changes, such as validation or real-time updates.

Checkboxes and RadioButtons are often used for multiple-choice selections. To respond to the user's choices, you can use setOnCheckedChangeListener for CheckBoxes and setOnCheckedChangeListener for RadioButtons:

```kotlin
val checkBox = findViewById<CheckBox>(R.id.checkBox)
checkBox.setOnCheckedChangeListener { _, isChecked ->
    if (isChecked) {
        // Checkbox is checked
    } else {
        // Checkbox is unchecked
    }
}

val radioButton = findViewById<RadioButton>(R.id.radioButton)
radioButton.setOnCheckedChangeListener { _, isChecked ->
    if (isChecked) {
        // RadioButton is selected
    }
}
```

Gestures and Touch Events

Android provides support for recognizing various gestures and touch events, such as swipes, pinch zoom, and long presses. You can implement gesture recognition by using GestureDetector or handling MotionEvent objects. Gestures can be especially useful for enhancing user experience in applications like games or multimedia apps.

Conclusion

Handling user interaction is a fundamental aspect of Android app development. By using event listeners like OnClickListener, TextWatcher, and OnCheckedChangeListener, you can capture and respond to user actions effectively. Understanding how to work with different user interface elements and their associated events is essential for creating interactive and user-friendly Android apps. In the following sections, we will explore adding functionality to your app and the process of debugging and testing it.

Section 3.3: Adding Functionality with Java/Kotlin

Building a user interface (UI) is just one part of developing an Android app. To create a functional app, you need to add logic and functionality to respond to user interactions and perform specific tasks. In this section, we'll explore how to add functionality to your Android app using Java or Kotlin.

Writing Code

Android app development primarily uses Java or Kotlin programming languages. You can write the logic and functionality for your app's components, such as Activities and Fragments, in these languages.

Here's an example of a simple Java method that performs a calculation:

```java
public int addNumbers(int num1, int num2) {
    return num1 + num2;
}
```

And the equivalent Kotlin function:

```kotlin
fun addNumbers(num1: Int, num2: Int): Int {
    return num1 + num2
}
```

You can place your code within the appropriate methods or functions in your Activity or Fragment classes.

Responding to User Actions

To make your app interactive, you'll often need to respond to user actions, such as button clicks or text input. You can achieve this by adding code within event listeners like OnClickListener, TextWatcher, and OnCheckedChangeListener, as discussed in the previous section (Section 3.2).

Here's an example of responding to a button click in Kotlin:

```kotlin
val button = findViewById<Button>(R.id.button)
button.setOnClickListener {
    // Code to execute when the button is clicked
    val result = addNumbers(5, 3)
    displayResult(result)
}
```

In this example, when the button is clicked, the addNumbers function is called, and the result is displayed using another function, displayResult.

Displaying Information

Displaying information to the user is a common task in app development. You can update TextViews, EditTexts, or other UI elements programmatically to show data or messages.

```
val textView = findViewById<TextView>(R.id.textView)
textView.text = "Hello, Android!"
```

In this example, we set the text of a TextView to "Hello, Android!" programmatically.

Implementing Business Logic

Apps often require more complex logic, such as data retrieval, processing, and storage. You can interact with databases, web services, or other data sources to fetch and manipulate data. Libraries like Retrofit and Room Database are commonly used for network requests and local data storage, respectively.

Debugging and Testing

As you add functionality to your app, it's essential to test and debug it thoroughly. Android Studio provides debugging tools that allow you to set breakpoints, inspect variables, and step through your code to identify and fix issues.

Additionally, unit testing and UI testing are essential for ensuring your app functions correctly. Android provides testing frameworks like JUnit and Espresso for writing and running tests.

Conclusion

Adding functionality to your Android app is a crucial step in turning a user interface into a fully operational application. You can write code in Java or Kotlin to respond to user interactions, implement business logic, and display information. Effective testing and debugging are essential to ensure your app works as intended. In the upcoming sections, we will explore debugging and running your app on a device or emulator, further enhancing your Android development skills.

Section 3.4: Debugging Your App

Debugging is a crucial part of Android app development. It's the process of identifying and fixing issues or errors in your code to ensure that your app runs smoothly. In this section, we'll explore various debugging techniques and tools available in Android Studio to help you debug your app effectively.

Setting Breakpoints

Breakpoints are markers that you can set in your code to pause program execution at a specific line. This allows you to inspect variables and step through your code to identify issues. To set a breakpoint in Android Studio, simply click on the left margin of the code editor next to the line where you want to pause execution.

```kotlin
fun calculateSum(a: Int, b: Int): Int {
    val result = a + b
    return result // Set a breakpoint here
}
```

When your app reaches the breakpoint, it will pause execution, and you can use the debugging tools to examine the state of your app.

Debugging Tools

Android Studio offers a comprehensive set of debugging tools to assist you during the debugging process. Some of the essential debugging tools include:

- **Debugger**: The core tool that allows you to inspect variables, evaluate expressions, and step through your code line by line.

- **Logcat**: Displays logs and messages generated by your app, which can be helpful for tracking the flow of your program and diagnosing issues.

- **Variables and Watches**: You can view and edit variable values and set watches to monitor specific variables during debugging.

- **Call Stack**: Shows the call hierarchy, allowing you to see how functions and methods are called.

- **Breakpoints**: You can manage breakpoints, enable or disable them, and set conditions for when they should trigger.

Running and Debugging

To run your app in debugging mode, click the "Debug" button in Android Studio instead of the regular "Run" button. This launches your app in debug mode, and you can interact with it as usual. When a breakpoint is reached, the app will pause, and you can use the debugging tools to inspect variables and the program's state.

Logging

Logging is an effective way to track the flow of your app and debug issues. You can use the Log class to print messages to the Logcat. For example:

```kotlin
import android.util.Log

...

Log.d("MyApp", "Debug message")
Log.e("MyApp", "Error message")
```

These log messages will appear in the Logcat, allowing you to monitor the execution of your app and catch potential problems.

Handling Exceptions

Exception handling is critical for robust app development. Android Studio provides tools to catch and handle exceptions during debugging. You can set breakpoints on exception types, inspect the exception details, and identify the root cause of crashes or unexpected behavior.

Profiling and Performance Optimization

In addition to debugging, Android Studio offers profiling tools that help you optimize your app's performance. Profiling allows you to monitor CPU, memory, and network usage, identify performance bottlenecks, and make necessary improvements.

Conclusion

Debugging is an integral part of Android app development. Android Studio provides a powerful set of debugging tools and features, including breakpoints, Logcat, variable inspection, and exception handling, to help you identify and resolve issues in your code. By mastering these debugging techniques, you can create more reliable and efficient Android apps. In the following sections, we will explore additional topics related to Android app development, including running your app on devices and handling user input and events.

Section 3.5: Running Your App on a Device

Running your Android app on a physical device or emulator is a crucial step in the development process. This allows you to test your app's functionality, user interface, and performance. In this section, we'll explore how to run your Android app on various devices and emulators using Android Studio.

Running on an Emulator

An Android emulator is a software-based virtual device that mimics the behavior of a physical Android device. It's an excellent tool for testing your app on different Android versions, screen sizes, and configurations.

1. **Create an Emulator**: In Android Studio, open the AVD Manager (Android Virtual Device Manager) by clicking "Tools" > "AVD Manager." Here, you can create and configure virtual devices (emulators) based on your testing needs.

2. **Start the Emulator**: Once you've created an emulator, you can start it by selecting it in the AVD Manager and clicking the "Play" button. It may take a few moments to boot up.

3. **Run Your App**: In Android Studio, select the emulator from the target device dropdown (next to the "Run" button). Click the "Run" button to deploy and launch your app on the emulator.

Testing your app on a physical Android device provides a more realistic user experience and allows you to check how your app performs on real hardware.

1. **Enable Developer Mode**: On your Android device, you need to enable Developer Mode. To do this, go to "Settings" > "About phone" > "Software information" and tap the "Build number" multiple times until you see a message indicating that Developer Mode is enabled.

2. **USB Debugging**: In the Developer Options, enable "USB debugging." This allows your computer to communicate with the device for debugging purposes.

3. **Connect Your Device**: Connect your Android device to your computer using a USB cable. Ensure that your computer recognizes the device.

4. **Select Your Device**: In Android Studio, select your connected device from the target device dropdown (next to the "Run" button).

5. **Run Your App**: Click the "Run" button to deploy and launch your app on the connected physical device.

When running your app on a device (either physical or virtual), you can use the debugging tools provided by Android Studio to set breakpoints, inspect variables, and debug issues in real-time. Debugging on a device is similar to debugging on an emulator.

While running your app during development, you use a debug version of the APK, which contains debugging information. When you're ready to release your app to the Play Store or distribute it to users, you need to build a release APK. Release APKs are optimized for performance and don't include debugging information.

To build a release APK, you can follow Android Studio's built-in tools for generating a signed APK. This process involves creating a signing key and configuring release build settings.

Running your Android app on both emulators and physical devices is a crucial part of the development process. It allows you to test your app's functionality, performance, and user experience across different Android versions and device configurations. Debugging on a device provides real-time insights into your app's behavior, making it easier to identify and resolve issues. When you're ready to release your app, building a release APK ensures optimal performance and security for your users. In the following chapters, we will delve deeper into various aspects of Android app development, including user interface design, data storage, networking, and more.

Chapter 4: User Interface Design in Android

Section 4.1: XML Layouts and Resources

User Interface (UI) design is a crucial aspect of Android app development. In this section, we'll explore the importance of XML layout files and resources in designing the visual components of your Android app.

XML Layouts

XML (Extensible Markup Language) is used in Android to define the layout and structure of your app's user interface. XML layout files are stored in the res/layout directory of your Android project. These files describe how UI elements are arranged and formatted.

For example, here's a basic XML layout for a login screen:

```xml
<?xml version="1.0" encoding="utf-8"?>
<LinearLayout
    xmlns:android="http://schemas.android.com/apk/res/android"
    android:layout_width="match_parent"
    android:layout_height="match_parent"
    android:orientation="vertical">

    <EditText
        android:id="@+id/usernameEditText"
        android:layout_width="match_parent"
        android:layout_height="wrap_content"
        android:hint="Username" />

    <EditText
        android:id="@+id/passwordEditText"
        android:layout_width="match_parent"
        android:layout_height="wrap_content"
        android:hint="Password"
        android:inputType="textPassword" />

    <Button
        android:id="@+id/loginButton"
        android:layout_width="wrap_content"
        android:layout_height="wrap_content"
        android:text="Login" />
</LinearLayout>
```

In this example, we use a LinearLayout as the root layout, which contains two EditText fields for username and password input and a Button for logging in.

Resource Files

Android allows you to separate resources, such as layout files, strings, images, and styles, from your code. This separation makes it easier to manage different aspects of your app's UI.

Resource files are stored in the `res` directory and organized into subdirectories like `res/layout` (for XML layouts), `res/values` (for strings and other values), `res/drawable` (for images), and more.

String Resources

String resources are often used to store text that appears in your app's UI. Defining strings in resource files allows for localization and makes it easier to update text across your app.

```xml
<!-- res/values/strings.xml -->
<resources>
    <string name="app_name">MyApp</string>
    <string name="login_button_text">Login</string>
</resources>
```

You can reference these strings in your XML layout files or code:

```xml
<!-- In an XML layout -->
<Button
    android:id="@+id/loginButton"
    android:layout_width="wrap_content"
    android:layout_height="wrap_content"
    android:text="@string/login_button_text" />
```

Dimension Resources

Dimension resources are used to store values like margins, padding, and text sizes. By defining dimensions in resource files, you can maintain consistency in your app's design.

```xml
<!-- res/values/dimens.xml -->
<resources>
    <dimen name="margin_large">16dp</dimen>
    <dimen name="text_size_medium">18sp</dimen>
</resources>
```

You can use these dimensions in your XML layout files:

```xml
<EditText
    android:id="@+id/usernameEditText"
    android:layout_width="match_parent"
    android:layout_height="wrap_content"
    android:layout_margin="@dimen/margin_large"
    android:textSize="@dimen/text_size_medium" />
```

Styles and themes allow you to define the appearance of UI elements consistently across your app. You can specify attributes like text color, background color, and text size in style and theme resources.

```xml
<!-- res/values/styles.xml -->
<resources>
    <style name="MyApp.EditTextStyle">
        <item name="android:textColor">@color/text_color</item>
        <item name="android:textSize">@dimen/text_size_medium</item>
    </style>
</resources>
```

You can apply styles to UI elements in your XML layout:

```xml
<EditText
    android:id="@+id/usernameEditText"
    style="@style/MyApp.EditTextStyle" />
```

Conclusion

XML layout files and resource files are essential components of Android UI design. They allow you to define the structure and appearance of your app's user interface in a structured and organized manner. By using resource files for strings, dimensions, styles, and themes, you can create consistent and easily maintainable UIs. In the upcoming sections, we will delve deeper into designing responsive layouts, working with widgets, themes, and accessibility considerations in Android app UI design.

Section 4.2: Designing Responsive Layouts

Designing responsive layouts in Android is crucial to ensure your app looks and functions well on various screen sizes and orientations. In this section, we'll explore the principles and techniques for creating responsive layouts that adapt to different devices.

ConstraintLayout

ConstraintLayout is a powerful layout manager that helps you create flexible and responsive UIs. It allows you to define relationships (constraints) between UI elements, enabling them to adapt dynamically to different screen sizes and orientations.

Key features of ConstraintLayout include:

- **Constraint Widgets**: Widgets are constrained to the layout's edges or to other widgets, specifying how they should be positioned relative to each other.

- **Guidelines**: Guidelines are horizontal or vertical lines that help you position UI elements consistently across different screen sizes.

- **Chains**: Chains allow you to group widgets and specify their alignment and spacing within the chain.

Here's an example of a simple ConstraintLayout:

```xml
<androidx.constraintlayout.widget.ConstraintLayout
    xmlns:android="http://schemas.android.com/apk/res/android"
    xmlns:app="http://schemas.android.com/apk/res-auto"
    xmlns:tools="http://schemas.android.com/tools"
    android:layout_width="match_parent"
    android:layout_height="match_parent"
    tools:context=".MainActivity">

    <Button
        android:id="@+id/button1"
        android:layout_width="wrap_content"
        android:layout_height="wrap_content"
        android:text="Button 1"
        app:layout_constraintStart_toStartOf="parent"
        app:layout_constraintTop_toTopOf="parent" />

    <Button
        android:id="@+id/button2"
        android:layout_width="wrap_content"
        android:layout_height="wrap_content"
        android:text="Button 2"
        app:layout_constraintEnd_toEndOf="parent"
        app:layout_constraintTop_toTopOf="parent" />

</androidx.constraintlayout.widget.ConstraintLayout>
```

In this example, we use ConstraintLayout to position two buttons at the top-left and top-right corners of the layout. The constraints ensure that the buttons adapt to different screen widths.

Supporting Multiple Screen Sizes

Android devices come in various screen sizes and densities, ranging from small phones to large tablets. To design responsive layouts, you can create different layout files for different screen sizes and orientations.

For example, you can have layout files for:

- `res/layout/main_activity.xml` (for default layout)
- `res/layout-sw600dp/main_activity.xml` (for tablets with a screen width of 600dp or more)

By providing alternative layouts for different screen sizes, you can tailor your app's UI to fit each device appropriately.

Supporting both landscape and portrait orientations is essential for a responsive design. You can create separate layout files for each orientation:

- `res/layout-land/main_activity.xml` (for landscape)
- `res/layout-port/main_activity.xml` (for portrait)

In these layout files, you can adjust the placement and size of UI elements to optimize the user experience in each orientation.

Dimension Qualifiers

In addition to layout files, you can use dimension qualifiers to define different sizes for resources like margins, padding, and text sizes based on screen size or density. This helps ensure that UI elements scale correctly on various devices.

For example:

- `res/values/dimens.xml` (for default dimensions)
- `res/values-sw600dp/dimens.xml` (for tablets with a screen width of 600dp or more)

In the dimension resource files, you can specify different values for dimensions to accommodate various screen sizes and densities.

Conclusion

Designing responsive layouts in Android involves using ConstraintLayout and creating alternative layout files and dimension resources to adapt to different screen sizes, orientations, and densities. By following responsive design principles, you can provide a consistent and user-friendly experience across a wide range of Android devices. In the next sections, we will explore working with widgets and views, as well as styling and theming your Android app for a polished and appealing UI.

Section 4.3: Working with Widgets and Views

Widgets and views are the building blocks of the user interface (UI) in Android apps. Understanding how to work with these components is essential for creating interactive and user-friendly interfaces. In this section, we'll explore widgets and views in Android app development.

What Are Widgets and Views?

- **Widgets**: In Android, widgets are UI elements that users can interact with, such as buttons, text fields, checkboxes, and radio buttons. Widgets allow users to input data, make selections, or trigger actions within the app.

- **Views**: Views are the fundamental building blocks of the UI hierarchy. Every visible element in an Android app is a subclass of the View class. Views are responsible for drawing content on the screen and handling user interaction.

Common UI Widgets

1. **Button**: Buttons are used to trigger actions when clicked by the user. They are often labeled with text, such as "Submit" or "Cancel."

2. **EditText**: EditText allows users to input text. It's commonly used for fields like username and password input.

3. **TextView**: TextView is used to display static or dynamic text. You can set its text programmatically or in XML layouts.

4. **CheckBox**: CheckBox is a UI element that allows users to toggle a binary choice, such as enabling or disabling a feature.

5. **RadioButton**: RadioButtons are typically used in groups where users can select one option from multiple choices.

6. **ImageView**: ImageView is used to display images or icons within your app's UI.

Working with Widgets in XML Layouts

To include widgets in your app's UI, you can define them in XML layout files. Here's an example of a simple layout with an EditText and a Button:

```
<LinearLayout
    xmlns:android="http://schemas.android.com/apk/res/android"
    android:layout_width="match_parent"
    android:layout_height="match_parent"
    android:orientation="vertical">

    <EditText
        android:id="@+id/editText"
        android:layout_width="match_parent"
        android:layout_height="wrap_content"
        android:hint="Enter your name" />

    <Button
        android:id="@+id/button"
        android:layout_width="wrap_content"
        android:layout_height="wrap_content"
        android:text="Submit" />
</LinearLayout>
```

In this XML layout, we have a LinearLayout that contains an EditText and a Button.

Working with Views Programmatically

You can also create and manipulate views programmatically using Java or Kotlin. For example, to create a TextView dynamically and add it to a LinearLayout:

```kotlin
val linearLayout = findViewById<LinearLayout>(R.id.linearLayout)

val textView = TextView(this)
textView.text = "Hello, World!"
textView.layoutParams = ViewGroup.LayoutParams(
    ViewGroup.LayoutParams.WRAP_CONTENT,
    ViewGroup.LayoutParams.WRAP_CONTENT
)

linearLayout.addView(textView)
```

This code creates a TextView, sets its text, and adds it to a LinearLayout defined in the XML layout.

Event Handling

To make your app interactive, you need to handle user interactions with widgets. You can do this by adding event listeners to widgets. For example, to handle a Button click event in Kotlin:

```kotlin
val button = findViewById<Button>(R.id.button)
button.setOnClickListener {
    // Handle button click
}
```

In this code, when the Button is clicked, the code inside the lambda expression is executed.

Custom Views

In addition to standard widgets, you can create custom views by extending the View class or its subclasses. Custom views allow you to create unique UI elements tailored to your app's requirements.

Conclusion

Widgets and views are fundamental components of Android app UIs. By understanding how to work with standard widgets, create custom views, and handle user interactions, you can design and build user-friendly and interactive interfaces for your Android apps. In the next sections, we will delve into topics such as themes, styles, accessibility, and more to enhance the overall user experience of your app.

Section 4.4: Themes and Styles

Themes and styles in Android are essential for maintaining a consistent and visually appealing user interface (UI) across your app. In this section, we'll explore the concepts of themes and styles and how to apply them to your Android app.

What Are Themes and Styles?

- **Themes**: A theme is a collection of attributes that define the look and feel of your app's UI. Themes specify colors, fonts, and other visual elements that create a consistent design across your app.

- **Styles**: Styles are sets of attributes that can be applied to individual UI elements, such as widgets and views. Styles allow you to define the appearance of specific components and reuse those definitions throughout your app.

Applying Themes

Android provides a set of predefined themes that you can apply to your app. Themes are defined in the `res/values/styles.xml` file. To apply a theme to your entire app, you specify it in the AndroidManifest.xml file as the app's theme:

```
<application
    ...
    android:theme="@style/AppTheme">
    ...
</application>
```

In this example, the `@style/AppTheme` theme is applied to the entire app. You can create custom themes in the `styles.xml` file by extending or modifying existing themes.

Creating Custom Styles

Custom styles allow you to define a set of attributes that can be applied to UI elements. To create a custom style, you define it in the `styles.xml` file, specifying the attributes you want to customize. Here's an example of a custom style that changes the text color and background color of a TextView:

```
<style name="MyTextViewStyle">
    <item name="android:textColor">#FF0000</item>
    <item name="android:background">#FFFF00</item>
</style>
```

You can then apply this style to a TextView in your XML layout:

```
<TextView
    android:id="@+id/myTextView"
    android:layout_width="wrap_content"
    android:layout_height="wrap_content"
```

```
    style="@style/MyTextViewStyle"
    android:text="Custom Styled Text" />
```

Inheritance and Overriding

Styles can inherit attributes from other styles. This allows you to create a base style and then create variations by overriding specific attributes. Here's an example of inheriting from a base style and overriding the text color:

```
<style name="MyButtonStyle" parent="Widget.AppCompat.Button">
    <item name="android:textColor">#00FF00</item>
</style>
```

Theme Attributes

Android provides a set of theme attributes that you can use to reference values defined in your themes and styles. For example, you can use `?android:attr/textColorPrimary` to reference the primary text color defined in the current theme.

```
<TextView
    android:layout_width="wrap_content"
    android:layout_height="wrap_content"
    android:text="Primary Text"
    android:textColor="?android:attr/textColorPrimary" />
```

This allows your UI elements to adapt to different themes without hardcoding specific colors.

Conclusion

Themes and styles are essential tools for creating a consistent and visually appealing UI in Android apps. By defining themes for your app and creating custom styles for specific UI elements, you can ensure a cohesive design across your application. Understanding theme attributes also allows your app's UI to adapt to different themes and maintain a professional appearance. In the following sections, we will explore accessibility considerations, best practices for UI design, and strategies for making your app user-friendly.

Section 4.5: Accessibility and Usability

Accessibility and usability are critical aspects of Android app development. Ensuring that your app is accessible to users with disabilities and provides a good user experience for all is essential. In this section, we'll explore the importance of accessibility and usability and how to implement best practices.

Android provides a range of accessibility features and guidelines to make apps more usable for individuals with disabilities. These features include screen readers, magnification gestures, and accessibility services.

Here are some key considerations for improving accessibility in your Android app:

1. **Content Descriptions**: Ensure that all images and interactive elements have meaningful content descriptions. Use the `android:contentDescription` attribute for images and other UI elements that require descriptions.

2. **Touch Targets**: Make interactive elements like buttons and links large enough to be easily tapped or clicked. This is particularly important for users with motor impairments.

3. **Text Size and Contrast**: Use legible text sizes and ensure sufficient contrast between text and background colors. This benefits users with visual impairments.

4. **Navigation**: Implement clear and consistent navigation structures. Use proper headings and labels for screen readers to provide context to users.

5. **Keyboard Navigation**: Ensure that your app can be fully navigated and interacted with using a keyboard or keyboard shortcuts.

6. **Testing with Accessibility Services**: Test your app with accessibility services enabled to identify and fix accessibility issues. Android provides tools like TalkBack for screen reading testing.

Usability Best Practices

In addition to accessibility, general usability principles are crucial for creating an engaging and user-friendly app:

1. **Intuitive Navigation**: Design your app's navigation in a logical and intuitive way. Users should be able to easily find their way around.

2. **Feedback and Error Handling**: Provide clear feedback to users when they perform actions or encounter errors. Error messages should be descriptive and actionable.

3. **Consistency**: Maintain a consistent visual design, layout, and interaction patterns throughout your app. This reduces cognitive load for users.

4. **Performance**: Optimize your app's performance to ensure smooth and responsive interactions. Slow or unresponsive apps frustrate users.

5. **Testing with Real Users**: Conduct usability testing with real users to identify pain points and areas for improvement. User feedback is invaluable.

6. **Internationalization and Localization**: If your app targets a global audience, support multiple languages and cultural preferences. This enhances the usability for users worldwide.

Android Accessibility Services

Android offers accessibility services like TalkBack, BrailleBack, and Switch Access to assist users with disabilities. These services provide various ways for users to interact with their devices, such as spoken feedback, braille displays, or switch input.

To ensure your app is compatible with these services, you should follow accessibility best practices and test your app with accessibility services enabled. Android Studio also provides accessibility checking tools to help you identify and fix issues.

Conclusion

Accessibility and usability are essential aspects of Android app development. By following accessibility guidelines and usability best practices, you can create apps that are inclusive and user-friendly. Ensuring that your app is accessible to users with disabilities and provides an excellent user experience for all users is not only a moral responsibility but also a legal requirement in many regions. In the upcoming sections, we will explore user input handling, validation, lists, and data storage in Android app development.

Chapter 5: User Input and Event Handling

Section 5.1: Handling User Touch and Gestures

Handling user touch input and gestures is a fundamental aspect of Android app development. In this section, we'll explore how to capture and respond to user interactions, including tapping, swiping, and gestures.

Understanding Touch Events

In Android, touch events are the primary way users interact with the screen. When a user touches the screen, the system generates touch events that your app can respond to. These touch events include:

- **ACTION_DOWN**: Fired when the user first touches the screen.
- **ACTION_MOVE**: Fired when the user's finger moves across the screen while touching it.
- **ACTION_UP**: Fired when the user lifts their finger from the screen.
- **ACTION_CANCEL**: Fired when the touch event is canceled, often due to a system event or interference.

To capture and respond to touch events, you can override the onTouchEvent method in your View or ViewGroup. Here's an example of handling a simple touch event in Kotlin:

```kotlin
override fun onTouchEvent(event: MotionEvent): Boolean {
    when (event.action) {
        MotionEvent.ACTION_DOWN -> {
            // User touched the screen
            return true // Consume the event
        }
        MotionEvent.ACTION_UP -> {
            // User lifted their finger
            return true // Consume the event
        }
        MotionEvent.ACTION_MOVE -> {
            // User's finger is moving on the screen
            return true // Consume the event
        }
        else -> return super.onTouchEvent(event)
    }
}
```

In this example, we respond to different touch event actions by checking event.action. Returning true indicates that the event is consumed, while returning false allows the event to propagate to other listeners.

Handling Multi-Touch Gestures

Android supports multi-touch gestures, allowing users to interact with the screen using multiple fingers simultaneously. Common multi-touch gestures include pinch-to-zoom and two-finger scrolling.

To handle multi-touch gestures, you can use the onTouchEvent method and the event.pointerCount property to determine the number of active touch points. Here's an example of handling a pinch-to-zoom gesture:

```kotlin
override fun onTouchEvent(event: MotionEvent): Boolean {
    when (event.actionMasked) {
        MotionEvent.ACTION_POINTER_DOWN -> {
            // A new pointer (finger) has touched the screen
            if (event.pointerCount == 2) {
                // Two fingers are now touching; this indicates a potential pinch-to-zoom gesture
                // Capture initial distance between the two fingers for scaling calculation
                initialDistance = calculateDistance(event)
                return true // Consume the event
            }
        }
        MotionEvent.ACTION_MOVE -> {
            if (event.pointerCount == 2) {
                // Two fingers are moving; calculate the current distance
                val currentDistance = calculateDistance(event)
                // Calculate the scaling factor based on the change in distance
                val scaleFactor = currentDistance / initialDistance
                // Apply scaling to your UI elements
                // ...
                // Update the initial distance for the next move event
                initialDistance = currentDistance
                return true // Consume the event
            }
        }
        MotionEvent.ACTION_POINTER_UP -> {
            // A pointer (finger) has been lifted
            if (event.pointerCount == 2) {
                // Two fingers are still on the screen; update initial distance
                initialDistance = calculateDistance(event)
            }
            return true // Consume the event
        }
    }
    return super.onTouchEvent(event)
}
```

```
private fun calculateDistance(event: MotionEvent): Float {
    val x = event.getX(0) - event.getX(1)
    val y = event.getY(0) - event.getY(1)
    return sqrt(x * x + y * y)
}
```

In this example, we capture multi-touch events to implement pinch-to-zoom behavior. We calculate the distance between two fingers to determine the scaling factor for zooming.

Gesture Detection

Android provides the GestureDetector class to simplify gesture detection. You can use it to detect common gestures like single tap, double tap, fling, and long press. Here's an example of using GestureDetector to detect a double-tap gesture:

```
val gestureDetector = GestureDetector(context, object : GestureDetector.Simpl
eOnGestureListener() {
    override fun onDoubleTap(e: MotionEvent): Boolean {
        // Handle double-tap gesture
        return true
    }
})

override fun onTouchEvent(event: MotionEvent): Boolean {
    gestureDetector.onTouchEvent(event)
    return true
}
```

In this example, we create a GestureDetector and override the onDoubleTap method to handle the double-tap gesture.

Conclusion

Handling user touch and gestures is vital for creating interactive and user-friendly Android apps. Understanding touch events, multi-touch gestures, and using gesture detection can enhance the user experience and enable users to interact naturally with your app. In the upcoming sections, we will explore capturing user input, keyboard handling, and validating user input in Android app development.

Section 5.2: Capturing User Input

Capturing user input is a fundamental aspect of Android app development. Apps often require user input for various purposes, such as data entry, form submission, and user interaction. In this section, we'll explore how to capture user input effectively in your Android app.

EditText Widget

The `EditText` widget is commonly used to capture text input from users. You can add an `EditText` widget to your layout XML file and access its content programmatically. Here's an example of how to define an `EditText` in XML:

```xml
<EditText
    android:id="@+id/editText"
    android:layout_width="match_parent"
    android:layout_height="wrap_content"
    android:hint="Enter your name" />
```

In this example, we've added an `EditText` widget with a hint text that provides a prompt to the user.

Accessing User Input

To access the text entered by the user in an `EditText` widget, you can use the `EditText` reference in your Java or Kotlin code. Here's an example in Kotlin:

```kotlin
val editText = findViewById<EditText>(R.id.editText)
val userInput = editText.text.toString()
```

In this code, we obtain a reference to the `EditText` using its ID (`R.id.editText`) and then retrieve the text entered by the user using the `text` property.

Handling User Input Events

In addition to capturing text, you can also handle user input events such as pressing the "Enter" key on the keyboard or detecting changes in text input. For example, you can listen for changes in the text and respond accordingly:

```kotlin
editText.addTextChangedListener(object : TextWatcher {
    override fun beforeTextChanged(s: CharSequence?, start: Int, count: Int,
after: Int) {
        // Called before text changes
    }

    override fun onTextChanged(s: CharSequence?, start: Int, before: Int, cou
nt: Int) {
        // Called when text changes
    }

    override fun afterTextChanged(s: Editable?) {
        // Called after text changes
    }
})
```

In this code, we add a `TextWatcher` to the `EditText` to listen for text changes. You can implement the appropriate actions in the `onTextChanged` or `afterTextChanged` methods.

Input Types and Validation

Android provides various input types for EditText widgets, such as text, numbers, passwords, emails, and more. You can specify the input type in XML or programmatically to ensure that the user enters data in the expected format.

For example, to set the input type to a numeric keyboard, you can use:

```xml
<EditText
    android:id="@+id/numericEditText"
    android:layout_width="match_parent"
    android:layout_height="wrap_content"
    android:hint="Enter a number"
    android:inputType="number" />
```

You can also perform input validation to ensure that user input meets specific criteria, such as minimum and maximum length, numeric values, or email format. Here's an example of validating user input for a password:

```kotlin
val passwordEditText = findViewById<EditText>(R.id.passwordEditText)
val password = passwordEditText.text.toString()

if (password.length < 8) {
    // Password is too short
    passwordEditText.error = "Password must be at least 8 characters long"
} else {
    // Password is valid
}
```

In this code, we check if the password is at least 8 characters long and display an error message if it's not.

Conclusion

Capturing user input is a crucial part of Android app development. By using EditText widgets, handling user input events, and applying input types and validation, you can create apps that effectively collect data and provide a seamless user experience. In the next sections, we will explore keyboard input handling and how to respond to various user events in your Android app.

Section 5.3: Handling Keyboard Input

Handling keyboard input is an essential aspect of Android app development, especially when dealing with text input fields. In this section, we'll explore how to manage the virtual keyboard, respond to keyboard events, and optimize the user experience.

Displaying the Virtual Keyboard

When a user interacts with an `EditText` widget or another text input field, the virtual keyboard automatically appears to allow text entry. Android manages the keyboard's appearance and disappearance based on the user's focus on input fields.

You can control the keyboard's behavior by specifying input types in your XML layout or programmatically. For example, to specify a numeric keyboard, you can use the `android:inputType` attribute:

```
<EditText
    android:id="@+id/numericEditText"
    android:layout_width="match_parent"
    android:layout_height="wrap_content"
    android:hint="Enter a number"
    android:inputType="number" />
```

Responding to Keyboard Events

To respond to keyboard events, you can implement listeners that capture key presses and key releases. Here's an example of listening for the "Enter" key press in an `EditText`:

```
val editText = findViewById<EditText>(R.id.editText)

editText.setOnKeyListener { _, keyCode, event ->
    if (keyCode == KeyEvent.KEYCODE_ENTER && event.action == KeyEvent.ACTION_UP) {
        // The Enter key was pressed
        // Handle the event here
        return@setOnKeyListener true
    }
    false
}
```

In this code, we set an `OnKeyListener` for the `EditText` to detect the "Enter" key press and handle it accordingly.

Hiding the Keyboard

There are situations where you might want to programmatically hide the virtual keyboard, such as after the user has finished entering text. To hide the keyboard, you can use the `InputMethodManager` class:

```
val imm = getSystemService(Context.INPUT_METHOD_SERVICE) as InputMethodManager
imm.hideSoftInputFromWindow(editText.windowToken, 0)
```

In this code, we obtain a reference to the `InputMethodManager` and call `hideSoftInputFromWindow` to hide the keyboard. You need to provide a window token (usually from an `EditText` or another view) to specify which input field's keyboard to hide.

When the virtual keyboard appears, it can cover parts of the screen, including input fields and buttons. To ensure a good user experience, you can adjust your layout to accommodate the keyboard.

You can set the `android:windowSoftInputMode` attribute in your activity's declaration in the AndroidManifest.xml file to specify how the window should behave when the keyboard appears. For example:

```
<activity
    android:name=".MyActivity"
    android:windowSoftInputMode="adjustResize">
    ...
</activity>
```

The `adjustResize` option adjusts the activity's layout to ensure that the focused input field is not obscured by the keyboard.

Conclusion

Handling keyboard input is essential for providing a seamless user experience in Android apps. By managing the virtual keyboard, responding to keyboard events, and adjusting your layout when necessary, you can create apps that are user-friendly and efficient for text input. In the following sections, we will explore more aspects of user input handling, including keyboard input validation and event handling.

Section 5.4: Responding to Events

In Android app development, responding to user events is a fundamental part of creating interactive and engaging applications. Events can be triggered by user actions like tapping buttons, scrolling, or swiping. In this section, we'll explore how to handle and respond to events in Android.

Event Listeners

To respond to user events, you need to set up event listeners or handlers for the UI elements you want to monitor. Event listeners are functions or classes that are called when a specific event occurs.

For example, you can set an `OnClickListener` for a button to respond to clicks:

```
val button = findViewById<Button>(R.id.myButton)

button.setOnClickListener {
    // Code to execute when the button is clicked
}
```

In this example, when the button is clicked, the code inside the lambda expression is executed.

In addition to setting event listeners, you can override specific event handling methods in your activity or fragment. These methods are automatically called when certain events occur. Some common event handling methods include:

- onCreate: Called when the activity is created.
- onStart: Called when the activity is about to become visible.
- onResume: Called when the activity is about to become interactive.
- onPause: Called when the activity is no longer in the foreground.
- onStop: Called when the activity is no longer visible.
- onDestroy: Called when the activity is destroyed.
- onBackPressed: Called when the back button is pressed.

You can override these methods to implement custom behavior in response to specific events.

Handling Click Events

Handling click events is one of the most common tasks in Android development. Buttons, image views, and other interactive elements often require click event handling. Here's an example of handling a click event for a button:

```
val button = findViewById<Button>(R.id.myButton)

button.setOnClickListener {
    // Code to execute when the button is clicked
    Toast.makeText(this, "Button clicked", Toast.LENGTH_SHORT).show()
}
```

In this code, a click listener is set for the button, and when the button is clicked, a toast message is displayed.

Handling Touch Events

If you need to respond to touch events, you can override the onTouchEvent method in your activity or custom view. This method receives motion events and allows you to implement custom touch behavior.

Here's an example of overriding onTouchEvent to detect touch events:

```
override fun onTouchEvent(event: MotionEvent): Boolean {
    when (event.action) {
        MotionEvent.ACTION_DOWN -> {
            // Finger touched the screen
            return true // Consume the event
        }
```

```
        MotionEvent.ACTION_MOVE -> {
            // Finger is moving on the screen
            return true // Consume the event
        }
        MotionEvent.ACTION_UP -> {
            // Finger lifted from the screen
            return true // Consume the event
        }
    }
    return super.onTouchEvent(event)
}
```

In this code, the onTouchEvent method responds to touch events and consumes them by returning true.

Conclusion

Event handling is a crucial part of creating interactive Android apps. By setting event listeners, overriding event handling methods, and responding to user actions, you can make your app dynamic and user-friendly. In the next sections, we will explore input validation, working with lists, and data storage in Android app development.

Section 5.5: Validating User Input

Validating user input is a critical aspect of Android app development to ensure data integrity and a smooth user experience. In this section, we'll explore techniques for validating user input and providing feedback to users when their input is incorrect or incomplete.

Why Input Validation Matters

Input validation helps prevent issues such as data corruption, application crashes, and security vulnerabilities. It ensures that the data entered by users conforms to expected formats and constraints. Proper input validation can also enhance user experience by providing clear feedback when input errors occur.

Using Input Types

Android provides various input types that can be set on EditText widgets to enforce specific input formats. For example:

- textEmailAddress: Ensures that the input is a valid email address.
- textPassword: Masks the input for password fields.
- number: Accepts only numeric input.

Here's an example of using an input type for an email address:

```
<EditText
    android:id="@+id/emailEditText"
    android:layout_width="match_parent"
    android:layout_height="wrap_content"
    android:hint="Enter your email"
    android:inputType="textEmailAddress" />
```

By specifying the input type, you inform the system about the expected format, which can trigger automatic validation and keyboard adjustments.

Implementing Custom Validation

In addition to input types, you may need to implement custom validation for specific input requirements. For instance, checking whether a password meets complexity criteria or verifying that a phone number has a valid format.

Here's an example of custom validation for a password field:

```
val passwordEditText = findViewById<EditText>(R.id.passwordEditText)
val password = passwordEditText.text.toString()

if (password.length < 8) {
    // Password is too short
    passwordEditText.error = "Password must be at least 8 characters long"
} else if (!password.matches(Regex(".*\\d.*"))) {
    // Password doesn't contain a digit
    passwordEditText.error = "Password must contain at least one digit"
} else {
    // Password is valid
}
```

In this code, we check the password's length and whether it contains at least one digit. If the password is invalid, we set an error message on the EditText to provide feedback to the user.

Displaying Error Messages

When input validation fails, it's important to display clear error messages to users. Android provides the setError method for EditText widgets to indicate input errors visually.

```
val editText = findViewById<EditText>(R.id.editText)
val userInput = editText.text.toString()

if (userInput.isEmpty()) {
    editText.error = "Field cannot be empty"
}
```

In this example, if the user leaves the input field empty, an error message is displayed below the EditText to inform the user of the problem.

Conclusion

Validating user input is essential for maintaining data integrity and ensuring a positive user experience in Android apps. Whether you use input types or implement custom validation, providing clear feedback to users when input errors occur is crucial. In the upcoming sections, we will explore working with lists, data storage, and networking in Android app development.

Chapter 6: Working with Lists and Adapters

Section 6.1: Creating Lists and Grids

In Android app development, working with lists and grids is a common requirement. Lists are used to display collections of data, such as contacts, messages, or products, in a scrollable format. Grids, on the other hand, are used to present data in a grid or matrix-like layout. This section focuses on creating and populating lists in Android using `ListView` and `RecyclerView` components.

Using ListView

`ListView` is a classic Android component for displaying lists. It's suitable for simple lists with a small number of items. To create a `ListView`, you typically follow these steps:

1. Define a layout for each item in the list. This layout will be inflated for each item in the list.

2. Create an adapter to bind your data to the `ListView`. The adapter manages the data and how it's displayed.

3. Set the adapter to the `ListView`.

Here's an example of creating a simple list using `ListView`:

```xml
<!-- item_layout.xml (Layout for each item) -->
<TextView
    xmlns:android="http://schemas.android.com/apk/res/android"
    android:id="@android:id/text1"
    android:layout_width="match_parent"
    android:layout_height="wrap_content"
    android:textAppearance="?android:attr/textAppearanceListItemSmall"
    android:gravity="center_vertical"
    android:paddingStart="?android:attr/listPreferredItemPaddingStart"
    android:paddingEnd="?android:attr/listPreferredItemPaddingEnd"
    android:minHeight="?android:attr/listPreferredItemHeightSmall"
    android:textColor="?android:attr/textColorPrimary" />
```

```java
// MainActivity.java
public class MainActivity extends AppCompatActivity {

    @Override
```

```java
    protected void onCreate(Bundle savedInstanceState) {
        super.onCreate(savedInstanceState);
        setContentView(R.layout.activity_main);

        // Sample data
        String[] data = {"Item 1", "Item 2", "Item 3", "Item 4", "Item 5"};

        // Create an ArrayAdapter to bind data to ListView
        ArrayAdapter<String> adapter = new ArrayAdapter<>(
            this,
            android.R.layout.simple_list_item_1, // Layout for each item
            data // Data to display
        );

        // Get the ListView
        ListView listView = findViewById(R.id.listView);

        // Set the adapter to the ListView
        listView.setAdapter(adapter);
    }
}
```

In this example, we define an item layout (`item_layout.xml`) and use an `ArrayAdapter` to populate a `ListView` with sample data.

Using RecyclerView

`RecyclerView` is a more flexible and powerful component for creating lists and grids. It's the recommended choice for displaying large datasets and custom layouts. To use `RecyclerView`, you need to perform these steps:

1. Define a layout for each item in the list, similar to the `ListView` approach.

2. Create an adapter that extends `RecyclerView.Adapter` to bind data to the `RecyclerView`. This adapter manages the data and the item views.

3. Set the adapter to the `RecyclerView`.

Here's an example of creating a list using `RecyclerView`:

```java
// MainActivity.java
public class MainActivity extends AppCompatActivity {

    @Override
    protected void onCreate(Bundle savedInstanceState) {
        super.onCreate(savedInstanceState);
        setContentView(R.layout.activity_main);

        // Sample data
        List<String> data = new ArrayList<>();
```

```java
        data.add("Item 1");
        data.add("Item 2");
        data.add("Item 3");
        data.add("Item 4");
        data.add("Item 5");

        // Get the RecyclerView
        RecyclerView recyclerView = findViewById(R.id.recyclerView);

        // Create an adapter for the RecyclerView
        MyAdapter adapter = new MyAdapter(data);

        // Set the adapter to the RecyclerView
        recyclerView.setAdapter(adapter);

        // Set the layout manager (e.g., LinearLayoutManager or GridLayoutMan
ager)
        recyclerView.setLayoutManager(new LinearLayoutManager(this));
    }
}

// MyAdapter.java
public class MyAdapter extends RecyclerView.Adapter<MyAdapter.ViewHolder> {

    private List<String> data;

    public MyAdapter(List<String> data) {
        this.data = data;
    }

    @NonNull
    @Override
    public ViewHolder onCreateViewHolder(@NonNull ViewGroup parent, int viewT
ype) {
        // Inflate the item layout and create a ViewHolder
        View view = LayoutInflater.from(parent.getContext())
            .inflate(R.layout.item_layout, parent, false);
        return new ViewHolder(view);
    }

    @Override
    public void onBindViewHolder(@NonNull ViewHolder holder, int position) {
        // Bind data to the ViewHolder
        holder.textView.setText(data.get(position));
    }

    @Override
    public int getItemCount() {
        return data.size();
```

```
    }

    public static class ViewHolder extends RecyclerView.ViewHolder {
        TextView textView;

        public ViewHolder(View itemView) {
            super(itemView);
            textView = itemView.findViewById(R.id.text1);
        }
    }
}
```

In this example, we create a `RecyclerView` and a custom adapter (`MyAdapter`) to populate it with data. The adapter inflates item views from the `item_layout.xml` and binds data to them.

Using `RecyclerView` offers more control and better performance when working with lists and grids in Android apps. It allows you to create complex layouts and efficiently handle large datasets.

Conclusion

Creating lists and grids is essential in many Android applications. You can choose between `ListView` and `RecyclerView` based on your specific requirements. `RecyclerView` is the preferred choice for more flexibility and performance, especially with larger datasets. In the upcoming sections, we'll explore customizing list views, handling item clicks, and implementing more advanced features in Android app development.

Section 6.2: Customizing List Views

In Android app development, customizing list views allows you to create visually appealing and user-friendly interfaces. You can tailor the appearance of list items, such as changing the layout, adding custom graphics, or providing interactive elements. This section explores various ways to customize list views in Android, focusing on `ListView` and `RecyclerView`.

Customizing `ListView` Items

Using Custom Layouts

One way to customize `ListView` items is by defining custom item layouts. You can create XML layout files for list items and then inflate these layouts in your adapter's `getView()` method. Here's an example:

```xml
<!-- custom_item_layout.xml -->
<LinearLayout xmlns:android="http://schemas.android.com/apk/res/android"
    android:layout_width="match_parent"
    android:layout_height="wrap_content"
    android:orientation="vertical">
```

```xml
<ImageView
    android:id="@+id/imageView"
    android:layout_width="wrap_content"
    android:layout_height="wrap_content"
    android:src="@drawable/ic_custom_image" />

<TextView
    android:id="@+id/textView"
    android:layout_width="wrap_content"
    android:layout_height="wrap_content"
    android:text="Custom Text"
    android:textSize="18sp" />
</LinearLayout>
```

In your adapter's getView() method:

```java
@Override
public View getView(int position, View convertView, ViewGroup parent) {
    if (convertView == null) {
        convertView = LayoutInflater.from(context).inflate(R.layout.custom_item_layout, parent, false);
    }

    ImageView imageView = convertView.findViewById(R.id.imageView);
    TextView textView = convertView.findViewById(R.id.textView);

    // Bind data to views based on the position
    imageView.setImageResource(data.get(position).getImageResource());
    textView.setText(data.get(position).getText());

    return convertView;
}
```

In this example, we create a custom item layout (custom_item_layout.xml) and inflate it in the adapter's getView() method. This allows you to customize the appearance of each list item.

Using Custom Adapters

Another way to customize ListView items is by creating custom adapters. By extending the BaseAdapter class or its subclasses, you have full control over how list items are created and displayed. Here's a simplified example:

```java
public class CustomAdapter extends BaseAdapter {

    private List<CustomData> data;
    private Context context;

    public CustomAdapter(Context context, List<CustomData> data) {
```

```java
        this.context = context;
        this.data = data;
    }

    @Override
    public int getCount() {
        return data.size();
    }

    @Override
    public Object getItem(int position) {
        return data.get(position);
    }

    @Override
    public long getItemId(int position) {
        return position;
    }

    @Override
    public View getView(int position, View convertView, ViewGroup parent) {
        // Implement your custom view creation logic here
        // You can reuse convertView for better performance

        View view = convertView;

        if (view == null) {
            LayoutInflater inflater = (LayoutInflater) context.getSystemServi
ce(Context.LAYOUT_INFLATER_SERVICE);
            view = inflater.inflate(R.layout.custom_item_layout, null);
        }

        ImageView imageView = view.findViewById(R.id.imageView);
        TextView textView = view.findViewById(R.id.textView);

        // Bind data to views based on the position
        imageView.setImageResource(data.get(position).getImageResource());
        textView.setText(data.get(position).getText());

        return view;
    }
}
```

In this example, we create a custom adapter (CustomAdapter) that extends BaseAdapter. It gives you fine-grained control over the list item views, allowing for extensive customization.

Customizing RecyclerView Items

Customizing RecyclerView items follows a similar approach as ListView, but it provides better performance and flexibility. You can define custom view holders and adapt the item views accordingly. Here's an example:

```java
public class CustomAdapter extends RecyclerView.Adapter<CustomAdapter.ViewHolder> {

    private List<CustomData> data;
    private Context context;

    public CustomAdapter(Context context, List<CustomData> data) {
        this.context = context;
        this.data = data;
    }

    @NonNull
    @Override
    public ViewHolder onCreateViewHolder(@NonNull ViewGroup parent, int viewType) {
        View view = LayoutInflater.from(context).inflate(R.layout.custom_item_layout, parent, false);
        return new ViewHolder(view);
    }

    @Override
    public void onBindViewHolder(@NonNull ViewHolder holder, int position) {
        holder.bind(data.get(position));
    }

    @Override
    public int getItemCount() {
        return data.size();
    }

    public class ViewHolder extends RecyclerView.ViewHolder {
        private ImageView imageView;
        private TextView textView;

        public ViewHolder(View itemView) {
            super(itemView);
            imageView = itemView.findViewById(R.id.imageView);
            textView = itemView.findViewById(R.id.textView);
        }

        public void bind(CustomData customData) {
            imageView.setImageResource(customData.getImageResource());
            textView.setText(customData.getText());
```

```
        }
    }
}
```

In this `RecyclerView` example, we define a custom adapter with a `ViewHolder` that binds data to views. The `onCreateViewHolder()` method inflates the custom item layout, and the `onBindViewHolder()` method binds data to the view holder.

Customizing list views in Android enhances the user experience and allows you to design unique interfaces. Whether you're using `ListView` or `RecyclerView`, understanding how to customize list items is a valuable skill in Android app development.

Section 6.3: Populating Lists with Data

Once you've set up your list view or recycler view and customized the items as needed, the next step is to populate these lists with data. In Android, you can source data from various places, such as arrays, databases, or network requests. This section explores different techniques for populating lists with data.

Populating a `ListView`

Using an Array Adapter

The simplest way to populate a `ListView` is by using an `ArrayAdapter`. You can create an `ArrayAdapter` and provide it with an array of data to display. Here's an example:

```java
// Sample data
String[] data = {"Item 1", "Item 2", "Item 3", "Item 4", "Item 5"};

// Create an ArrayAdapter to bind data to ListView
ArrayAdapter<String> adapter = new ArrayAdapter<>(
    this,
    android.R.layout.simple_list_item_1, // Layout for each item
    data // Data to display
);

// Get the ListView
ListView listView = findViewById(R.id.listView);

// Set the adapter to the ListView
listView.setAdapter(adapter);
```

In this example, we create an `ArrayAdapter` and provide it with an array of strings. The adapter takes care of displaying the data in the `ListView`.

Using a Custom Adapter

If your data is more complex and doesn't fit neatly into a string array, you can create a custom adapter, as shown in the previous section. With a custom adapter, you have full control over how data is bound to list items. You can source data from databases, APIs, or any other data store.

Populating a `RecyclerView`

Using a Custom Adapter

For populating a `RecyclerView`, using a custom adapter is the recommended approach. It allows you to efficiently manage data binding and view recycling. Here's an example:

```
// Sample data
List<CustomData> data = getDataFromSource(); // Replace with your data source

// Get the RecyclerView
RecyclerView recyclerView = findViewById(R.id.recyclerView);

// Create an adapter for the RecyclerView
CustomAdapter adapter = new CustomAdapter(this, data);

// Set the adapter to the RecyclerView
recyclerView.setAdapter(adapter);

// Set the layout manager (e.g., LinearLayoutManager or GridLayoutManager)
recyclerView.setLayoutManager(new LinearLayoutManager(this));
```

In this example, we create a custom adapter (`CustomAdapter`) and provide it with a list of custom data objects. The adapter handles data binding and view recycling efficiently.

Loading Data from External Sources

In real-world Android applications, you often need to load data from external sources like APIs or databases. To do this, you can use background threads or libraries like Retrofit for network requests. Make sure to load data asynchronously to avoid blocking the UI thread.

Updating Data Dynamically

In many cases, you might need to update the data displayed in your list dynamically. To achieve this, you can update the underlying data source (e.g., an array or a list) and then notify the adapter of the data change using methods like `notifyDataSetChanged()` for `ArrayAdapter` or `notifyItemInserted()`, `notifyItemRemoved()`, or `notifyItemChanged()` for `RecyclerView.Adapter`. This triggers a refresh of the list view with the updated data.

```
// Example of updating data in a RecyclerView
data.add(newItem); // Add a new item to the data source
adapter.notifyItemInserted(data.size() - 1); // Notify the adapter of the change
```

Conclusion

Populating lists with data is a fundamental aspect of Android app development. Whether you're using a `ListView` or a `RecyclerView`, understanding how to source and display data is crucial for creating functional and engaging apps. Be mindful of performance considerations, especially when dealing with large datasets, and make use of background threads when loading data from external sources.

Section 6.4: Handling Item Clicks and Selections

In Android app development, handling item clicks and selections in lists (whether using `ListView` or `RecyclerView`) is a common requirement. Users expect to interact with the items they see on the screen. This section explores how to respond to item clicks and selections in Android.

Handling Item Clicks in `ListView`

Using OnItemClickListener

To handle item clicks in a `ListView`, you can set an `OnItemClickListener` on the `ListView` instance. Here's an example:

```java
ListView listView = findViewById(R.id.listView);

listView.setOnItemClickListener(new AdapterView.OnItemClickListener() {
    @Override
    public void onItemClick(AdapterView<?> parent, View view, int position, long id) {
        // Handle the item click here
        String selectedItem = (String) parent.getItemAtPosition(position);
        Toast.makeText(getApplicationContext(), "Clicked: " + selectedItem, Toast.LENGTH_SHORT).show();
    }
});
```

In this example, we set an `OnItemClickListener` on the `ListView`. When an item is clicked, the `onItemClick` method is invoked, allowing you to perform actions based on the clicked item.

Handling Item Clicks in `RecyclerView`

Using Interface Callbacks

In a `RecyclerView`, you can handle item clicks by defining an interface and implementing it in your `RecyclerView.Adapter`. Here's an example:

```java
public interface OnItemClickListener {
    void onItemClick(int position);
```

```
}

public class CustomAdapter extends RecyclerView.Adapter<CustomAdapter.ViewHol
der> {
    private List<CustomData> data;
    private OnItemClickListener listener;

    // Constructor to set the listener
    public CustomAdapter(List<CustomData> data, OnItemClickListener listener)
{
        this.data = data;
        this.listener = listener;
    }

    // ViewHolder and other adapter methods...

    @Override
    public void onBindViewHolder(@NonNull ViewHolder holder, final int positi
on) {
        // Bind data to views
        holder.bind(data.get(position));

        // Set a click listener on the item view
        holder.itemView.setOnClickListener(new View.OnClickListener() {
            @Override
            public void onClick(View v) {
                if (listener != null) {
                    listener.onItemClick(position);
                }
            }
        });
    }
}
```

In this example, we define an `OnItemClickListener` interface and pass it to the `CustomAdapter`. In the `onBindViewHolder` method, we set a click listener on the item view and invoke the `onItemClick` method of the listener when an item is clicked.

Using ItemDecoration

Another way to handle item clicks in a `RecyclerView` is by using `ItemDecoration` with `RecyclerView.SimpleOnItemTouchListener`. This approach allows you to attach a click listener directly to the `RecyclerView` and determine which item was clicked based on the touch coordinates.

```
public class RecyclerViewItemClickListener implements RecyclerView.OnItemTouc
hListener {
    private OnItemClickListener listener;
    private GestureDetector gestureDetector;
```

```java
    public RecyclerViewItemClickListener(Context context, final RecyclerView
recyclerView, final OnItemClickListener listener) {
        this.listener = listener;
        gestureDetector = new GestureDetector(context, new GestureDetector.Si
mpleOnGestureListener() {
            @Override
            public boolean onSingleTapUp(MotionEvent e) {
                return true;
            }
        });

        recyclerView.addOnItemTouchListener(this);
    }

    @Override
    public boolean onInterceptTouchEvent(@NonNull RecyclerView rv, @NonNull M
otionEvent e) {
        View child = rv.findChildViewUnder(e.getX(), e.getY());
        if (child != null && listener != null && gestureDetector.onTouchEvent
(e)) {
            listener.onItemClick(rv.getChildAdapterPosition(child));
            return true;
        }
        return false;
    }

    @Override
    public void onTouchEvent(@NonNull RecyclerView rv, @NonNull MotionEvent e
) {
    }

    @Override
    public void onRequestDisallowInterceptTouchEvent(boolean disallowIntercep
t) {
    }
}
```

In this example, we create a `RecyclerViewItemClickListener` that listens for single taps on items in the `RecyclerView`. It uses a `GestureDetector` to determine if a click occurred and invokes the `onItemClick` method of the listener.

Handling Item Selection

In addition to item clicks, you might also need to handle item selection, especially in multi-select scenarios. You can maintain a list of selected items and update the UI accordingly. Implementing item selection depends on your app's requirements and can involve checkboxes, highlighting, or other UI elements.

Conclusion

Handling item clicks and selections in lists is essential for creating interactive and user-friendly Android apps. Whether you're working with `ListView` or `RecyclerView`, understanding how to respond to user interactions with list items is a fundamental skill in Android app development. Choose the approach that best suits your app's needs and user experience.

Section 6.5: Implementing Recycler Views

Recycler Views are a powerful and efficient way to display lists or grids of data in Android apps. They are more flexible and performant than the older `ListView` and offer better support for handling large datasets. In this section, we'll explore how to implement Recycler Views in your Android application.

Setting Up a Recycler View

To get started with a Recycler View, you'll need to follow these steps:

1. **Add the Recycler View to Your Layout**: In your XML layout file, add a `RecyclerView` element where you want the list to appear. For example:

```
<androidx.recyclerview.widget.RecyclerView
    android:id="@+id/recyclerView"
    android:layout_width="match_parent"
    android:layout_height="match_parent"
    android:scrollbars="vertical"
    />
```

2. **Create a Custom Adapter**: You'll need to create a custom adapter class that extends `RecyclerView.Adapter`. This adapter is responsible for binding your data to the views in the list. You can also create a custom view holder class that extends `RecyclerView.ViewHolder` to hold references to the views in each item.

```
public class CustomAdapter extends RecyclerView.Adapter<CustomAdapter.ViewHolder> {
    // Define your data source and methods for binding data here

    @NonNull
    @Override
    public ViewHolder onCreateViewHolder(@NonNull ViewGroup parent, int viewType) {
        // Inflate your item layout and create a ViewHolder
        View view = LayoutInflater.from(parent.getContext()).inflate(R.layout.item_layout, parent, false);
        return new ViewHolder(view);
    }

    @Override
```

```java
public void onBindViewHolder(@NonNull ViewHolder holder, int position) {
    // Bind data to your ViewHolder's views here
}

@Override
public int getItemCount() {
    // Return the number of items in your data source
    return dataList.size();
}

public class ViewHolder extends RecyclerView.ViewHolder {
    // Declare views in your item layout here

    public ViewHolder(@NonNull View itemView) {
        super(itemView);
        // Initialize views here
    }
}
}
```

3. **Initialize and Set the Adapter**: In your activity or fragment, initialize the Recycler View, create an instance of your custom adapter, and set it to the Recycler View.

```java
RecyclerView recyclerView = findViewById(R.id.recyclerView);
CustomAdapter adapter = new CustomAdapter(dataList); // Pass your data source
to the adapter
recyclerView.setAdapter(adapter);
```

4. **Layout Manager**: Choose and set a layout manager for your Recycler View. The layout manager is responsible for positioning items in the list, and you can use either LinearLayoutManager, GridLayoutManager, or a custom layout manager based on your design requirements.

```java
recyclerView.setLayoutManager(new LinearLayoutManager(this));
```

Handling Clicks and Interactions

Handling item clicks in a Recycler View was covered in Section 6.4. You can use either OnItemClickListener, interface callbacks, or ItemDecoration to handle clicks based on your app's needs.

Performance Optimization

Recycler Views are designed for efficient handling of large datasets. To ensure smooth scrolling and responsiveness, consider implementing the following:

- **View Recycling**: Recycler Views automatically recycle item views that are no longer visible, which saves memory and improves performance.

- **Pagination**: If you have a large dataset, consider implementing pagination to load data in chunks as the user scrolls.

- **Async Loading**: For loading data from external sources, use background threads or libraries like Retrofit to avoid blocking the UI thread.

- **Data Binding**: Consider using data binding to bind data to views more efficiently.

- **View Type**: If your Recycler View contains different types of items, override `getItemViewType()` in your adapter to handle multiple view types.

Customizing Item Layouts

Each item in a Recycler View can have a different layout, allowing you to create complex and dynamic lists. You can use different XML layout files for different item types and inflate them based on the item's position or type in the `onCreateViewHolder()` method of your adapter.

Conclusion

Recycler Views are a versatile and essential component in Android app development, particularly when dealing with lists or grids of data. Understanding how to set up and customize Recycler Views, along with handling item clicks and optimizing performance, is crucial for creating responsive and user-friendly apps.

Chapter 7: Data Storage and Persistence

Section 7.1: Saving Data in SharedPreferences

Android apps often need to store and retrieve user-specific settings and small pieces of data persistently. SharedPreferences is a simple and convenient way to accomplish this. In this section, we'll explore how to use SharedPreferences for data storage in your Android app.

Introduction to SharedPreferences

SharedPreferences is a key-value storage mechanism provided by Android. It allows you to store simple data types such as strings, integers, booleans, and floats. SharedPreferences are often used for storing user preferences, settings, and other small pieces of data that need to persist across app sessions.

Getting a SharedPreferences Instance

To use SharedPreferences, you first need to obtain an instance associated with your app's context. You can do this using the `getSharedPreferences()` method:

```
SharedPreferences sharedPreferences = getSharedPreferences("my_prefs", Context.MODE_PRIVATE);
```

In this example, we create a SharedPreferences instance named "my_prefs." The second argument, `Context.MODE_PRIVATE`, indicates that the data can only be accessed by the calling app and is stored in a private file.

Storing Data

You can store data in SharedPreferences using the various `put` methods based on the data type you want to store. For example:

```
SharedPreferences.Editor editor = sharedPreferences.edit();
editor.putString("username", "john_doe");
editor.putInt("user_age", 30);
editor.putBoolean("is_logged_in", true);
editor.apply(); // Apply changes
```

In this example, we use `putString()`, `putInt()`, and `putBoolean()` to store a username, age, and login status, respectively. Changes are committed by calling `apply()` or `commit()` on the `SharedPreferences.Editor` instance.

Retrieving Data

To retrieve data from SharedPreferences, you can use the corresponding `get` methods based on the data type:

```
String username = sharedPreferences.getString("username", "");
int userAge = sharedPreferences.getInt("user_age", 0);
boolean isLoggedIn = sharedPreferences.getBoolean("is_logged_in", false);
```

In this example, we retrieve the previously stored values, providing default values as the second argument in case the key is not found.

Removing Data

You can remove data from SharedPreferences using the `remove()` method:

```
SharedPreferences.Editor editor = sharedPreferences.edit();
editor.remove("username");
editor.apply(); // Apply changes
```

This will remove the "username" key and its associated value from SharedPreferences.

Conclusion

SharedPreferences offer a straightforward way to store and retrieve simple data persistently in Android apps. They are suitable for storing user preferences, settings, and other small pieces of data that need to be retained between app sessions. However, for more complex data storage requirements, such as structured data or large datasets, other storage options like SQLite databases or file storage may be more appropriate.

Section 7.2: Using Internal Storage

Internal storage is one of the primary ways to store private app-specific data on an Android device. In this section, we'll explore how to use internal storage to store and retrieve data in your Android app.

What Is Internal Storage?

Internal storage refers to a private storage area within your app's sandboxed environment. It's not directly accessible by other apps or users, making it a secure location for storing sensitive data or files that are specific to your app. Internal storage is particularly useful for storing application data that should not be visible or editable by users.

Saving Data to Internal Storage

To save data to internal storage, you need to use the file system provided by Android. Here are the basic steps to save data:

1. **Open or Create a File**: You can use the `openFileOutput()` method to create or open a file for writing. This method returns a `FileOutputStream` that you can use to write data to the file.

```
String filename = "my_data.txt";
String content = "This is my data to save.";
```

```
try {
    FileOutputStream fos = openFileOutput(filename, Context.MODE_PRIVATE);
    fos.write(content.getBytes());
    fos.close();
} catch (IOException e) {
    e.printStackTrace();
}
```

In this example, we create a file named "my_data.txt" and write the content to it. The `Context.MODE_PRIVATE` flag ensures that the file is private to your app.

2. **Write Data**: You can use the `write()` method of the `FileOutputStream` to write data to the file. In this case, we write the content as bytes by converting it to a byte array.

3. **Close the File**: Always remember to close the `FileOutputStream` to release system resources.

Reading Data from Internal Storage

To read data from internal storage, follow these steps:

1. **Open the File**: Use the `openFileInput()` method to open an existing file for reading. It returns a `FileInputStream` for reading data from the file.

```
String filename = "my_data.txt";

try {
    FileInputStream fis = openFileInput(filename);
    InputStreamReader isr = new InputStreamReader(fis);
    BufferedReader br = new BufferedReader(isr);
    StringBuilder stringBuilder = new StringBuilder();
    String line;

    while ((line = br.readLine()) != null) {
        stringBuilder.append(line).append("\n");
    }

    fis.close();
    String content = stringBuilder.toString();
} catch (IOException e) {
    e.printStackTrace();
}
```

In this code, we open the file "my_data.txt" for reading and use a `BufferedReader` to read the file line by line.

2. **Read Data**: Read data from the `FileInputStream` using the `readLine()` method or other methods based on your data format.

3. **Close the File**: Always close the `FileInputStream` and other related resources after reading.

Internal storage provides a secure and private location for your app to store and retrieve data. It's suitable for storing small to moderate amounts of application-specific data, such as configuration settings, user preferences, or data files. When working with larger datasets or structured data, you may consider using other storage options like SQLite databases or external storage.

Section 7.3: Working with External Storage

External storage provides a shared storage location that's accessible to other apps and users. It's useful for storing files that need to be shared between apps or data that users may want to access directly. In this section, we'll explore how to work with external storage in your Android app.

Understanding External Storage

External storage can be either removable (e.g., SD cards) or non-removable (internal storage that's shared with other apps). It offers more space than internal storage and is ideal for storing large files, media, and data that users may want to transfer between devices or access using other apps.

Checking External Storage Availability

Before working with external storage, it's essential to check if it's available on the device and if your app has permission to access it. You can use the following code to check for external storage availability:

```
String state = Environment.getExternalStorageState();

if (Environment.MEDIA_MOUNTED.equals(state)) {
    // External storage is available and writable
} else if (Environment.MEDIA_MOUNTED_READ_ONLY.equals(state)) {
    // External storage is available but read-only
} else {
    // External storage is not available
}
```

In this code, we use `Environment.getExternalStorageState()` to get the current state of external storage. If it equals `Environment.MEDIA_MOUNTED`, external storage is available and writable. If it equals `Environment.MEDIA_MOUNTED_READ_ONLY`, it's available but read-only. In all other cases, external storage is not available.

Writing to External Storage

To write data to external storage, you need to request the appropriate permission in your AndroidManifest.xml file:

```
<uses-permission android:name="android.permission.WRITE_EXTERNAL_STORAGE" />
```

Then, you can use the following code to write data to external storage:

```
File directory = Environment.getExternalStoragePublicDirectory(Environment.DI
RECTORY_DOCUMENTS);
File file = new File(directory, "my_file.txt");

try {
    FileOutputStream fos = new FileOutputStream(file);
    String content = "This is data written to external storage.";
    fos.write(content.getBytes());
    fos.close();
} catch (IOException e) {
    e.printStackTrace();
}
```

In this example, we specify the target directory using
Environment.getExternalStoragePublicDirectory(). You can choose from various predefined directories like DIRECTORY_DOCUMENTS, DIRECTORY_PICTURES, etc., based on the type of data you are storing.

Reading from External Storage

Reading data from external storage is similar to reading from internal storage. You can use a FileInputStream to read data from a file located in the external storage directory:

```
File directory = Environment.getExternalStoragePublicDirectory(Environment.DI
RECTORY_DOCUMENTS);
File file = new File(directory, "my_file.txt");

try {
    FileInputStream fis = new FileInputStream(file);
    InputStreamReader isr = new InputStreamReader(fis);
    BufferedReader br = new BufferedReader(isr);
    StringBuilder stringBuilder = new StringBuilder();
    String line;

    while ((line = br.readLine()) != null) {
        stringBuilder.append(line).append("\n");
    }

    fis.close();
    String content = stringBuilder.toString();
} catch (IOException e) {
```

```
        e.printStackTrace();
    }
```

Working with external storage in Android allows your app to store data that can be accessed and shared by other apps and users. However, it's essential to handle external storage with care, request the necessary permissions, and check for availability to ensure a smooth and secure user experience.

Section 7.4: SQLite Databases in Android

SQLite databases are a powerful and efficient way to store structured data in Android apps. In this section, we'll explore how to work with SQLite databases, from creating and managing databases to performing CRUD (Create, Read, Update, Delete) operations on data.

Introduction to SQLite Databases

SQLite is a lightweight, serverless, and self-contained database engine that is used extensively in Android for local data storage. It's embedded within the Android framework, making it a natural choice for data storage in Android apps.

SQLite databases are ideal for structured data, such as user profiles, product catalogs, or application logs. They offer ACID (Atomicity, Consistency, Isolation, Durability) compliance, ensuring data integrity even in complex scenarios.

Creating a SQLite Database

To create a SQLite database in your Android app, you need to extend the SQLiteOpenHelper class. Here's a basic example of how to create a database:

```java
public class MyDatabaseHelper extends SQLiteOpenHelper {
    private static final String DATABASE_NAME = "my_app.db";
    private static final int DATABASE_VERSION = 1;

    public MyDatabaseHelper(Context context) {
        super(context, DATABASE_NAME, null, DATABASE_VERSION);
    }

    @Override
    public void onCreate(SQLiteDatabase db) {
        // Create the database tables and define their schema here
        String createTableSQL = "CREATE TABLE IF NOT EXISTS users " +
                "(id INTEGER PRIMARY KEY AUTOINCREMENT, " +
                "username TEXT, " +
                "email TEXT)";
        db.execSQL(createTableSQL);
    }
```

```java
    @Override
    public void onUpgrade(SQLiteDatabase db, int oldVersion, int newVersion)
{
        // Handle database schema upgrades here
        if (oldVersion < newVersion) {
            db.execSQL("DROP TABLE IF EXISTS users");
            onCreate(db);
        }
    }
}
```

In this example, we create a MyDatabaseHelper class that extends SQLiteOpenHelper. We define the database name and version, and in the onCreate() method, we specify the database schema by executing SQL statements to create tables.

Performing CRUD Operations

SQLite databases support the standard CRUD operations:

1. **Create**: Insert new data into the database.

2. **Read**: Retrieve data from the database.

3. **Update**: Modify existing data in the database.

4. **Delete**: Remove data from the database.

Here are examples of how to perform these operations:

Create (Insert Data):
```java
SQLiteDatabase db = myDatabaseHelper.getWritableDatabase();
ContentValues values = new ContentValues();
values.put("username", "john_doe");
values.put("email", "john@example.com");
long newRowId = db.insert("users", null, values);
```

Read (Query Data):
```java
SQLiteDatabase db = myDatabaseHelper.getReadableDatabase();
String[] projection = {"id", "username", "email"};
Cursor cursor = db.query("users", projection, null, null, null, null, null);

while (cursor.moveToNext()) {
    int userId = cursor.getInt(cursor.getColumnIndex("id"));
    String username = cursor.getString(cursor.getColumnIndex("username"));
    String email = cursor.getString(cursor.getColumnIndex("email"));
    // Process retrieved data here
}
cursor.close();
```

Update (Modify Data):
```
SQLiteDatabase db = myDatabaseHelper.getWritableDatabase();
ContentValues values = new ContentValues();
values.put("email", "new_email@example.com");
int rowsUpdated = db.update("users", values, "username=?", new String[]{"john
_doe"});
```

Delete (Remove Data):
```
SQLiteDatabase db = myDatabaseHelper.getWritableDatabase();
int rowsDeleted = db.delete("users", "username=?", new String[]{"john_doe"});
```

Conclusion

SQLite databases are a versatile and efficient way to store structured data in Android apps. They offer transactional support and are well-suited for various use cases, from simple data storage to more complex scenarios. When designing your app's database schema, consider the specific data requirements and relationships to create an efficient and maintainable database structure.

Section 7.5: Data Backup and Restore

Data backup and restore mechanisms are crucial for ensuring that user data is safe and can be recovered in case of device loss, data corruption, or app reinstallation. In this section, we'll explore strategies for implementing data backup and restore features in your Android app.

Importance of Data Backup

Users rely on their apps to store essential data, such as notes, settings, or documents. Losing this data can be a significant inconvenience. Therefore, providing a data backup and restore feature can greatly enhance the user experience and build trust in your app.

Android Backup Service

Android provides a built-in backup service that allows your app to back up data to the user's Google Drive account. This service is available on devices running Android 6.0 (API level 23) and higher. Here's how to use it:

1. **Declare Backup Behavior**: In your app's AndroidManifest.xml file, declare the backup behavior using the `<application>` element:
```
<application
    android:allowBackup="true"
    android:fullBackupContent="@xml/my_backup_rules"
    ...>
    ...
</application>
```

The `android:allowBackup` attribute should be set to `true` to enable backup, and `android:fullBackupContent` points to an XML resource file that defines which files and data to include in the backup.

2. **Define Backup Rules**: Create a backup rules XML file (e.g., `my_backup_rules.xml`) that specifies what data to include or exclude from backups. For example:

```xml
<?xml version="1.0" encoding="utf-8"?>
<full-backup-content>
    <!-- Include app's shared preferences -->
    <include domain="sharedpref" path="my_app_prefs.xml" />
    <!-- Exclude cache files -->
    <exclude domain="cache" />
</full-backup-content>
```

3. **Implement Backup Data**: In your app, you can implement the `BackupAgent` class to define how data is backed up. This class handles backup and restore operations.

```java
public class MyBackupAgent extends BackupAgentHelper {
    @Override
    public void onCreate() {
        SharedPreferencesBackupHelper helper = new SharedPreferencesBackupHelper(this, "my_app_prefs");
        addHelper("my_prefs", helper);
    }
}
```

4. **Trigger Backup**: To trigger a backup, you can use the `BackupManager`:

```java
BackupManager backupManager = new BackupManager(context);
backupManager.dataChanged();
```

Data Restore

Data restoration is typically handled automatically by Android when a user reinstalls your app on a new device or after a factory reset. Android will restore the app's data from the user's Google Drive backup, preserving their settings and data.

Conclusion

Implementing data backup and restore features in your Android app helps ensure that users don't lose important data and settings. By following Android's backup guidelines and using the built-in backup service, you can provide a seamless and reliable backup experience for your users.

Chapter 8: Networking and Internet Connectivity

Section 8.1: Making HTTP Requests

In modern Android app development, network connectivity is a fundamental requirement. Apps often need to fetch data from remote servers, interact with APIs, or send data to a backend server. To achieve this, you'll need to make HTTP requests from your Android app. In this section, we'll explore the techniques and best practices for making HTTP requests in Android.

Android's HTTP Libraries

Android provides several ways to perform HTTP requests, and the choice of library depends on your specific requirements. Two commonly used libraries are HttpURLConnection and the more modern OkHttp. Here's an overview of both:

HttpURLConnection

HttpURLConnection is a built-in Java class that provides a basic way to perform HTTP requests. While it's available by default and suitable for simple use cases, it's relatively low-level and may require more code to achieve the same functionality as other libraries.

Here's a simple example of making an HTTP GET request using HttpURLConnection:

```java
try {
    URL url = new URL("https://api.example.com/data");
    HttpURLConnection connection = (HttpURLConnection) url.openConnection();

    // Set request method to GET
    connection.setRequestMethod("GET");

    // Read the response
    int responseCode = connection.getResponseCode();
    if (responseCode == HttpURLConnection.HTTP_OK) {
        InputStream inputStream = connection.getInputStream();
        // Read and process the response data
    } else {
        // Handle the error
    }

    connection.disconnect();
} catch (IOException e) {
    e.printStackTrace();
}
```

OkHttp

OkHttp is a popular and efficient HTTP client for Android. It provides a higher-level API, automatic connection pooling, and other features, making it a preferred choice for most Android developers.

To use OkHttp, you'll need to include its dependency in your app's build.gradle file:

```
implementation 'com.squareup.okhttp3:okhttp:4.9.1'
```

Here's an example of making an HTTP GET request using OkHttp:

```
OkHttpClient client = new OkHttpClient();
Request request = new Request.Builder()
        .url("https://api.example.com/data")
        .build();

try (Response response = client.newCall(request).execute()) {
    if (response.isSuccessful()) {
        String responseData = response.body().string();
        // Process the response data
    } else {
        // Handle the error
    }
} catch (IOException e) {
    e.printStackTrace();
}
```

Handling Asynchronous Requests

Network requests should be made asynchronously to avoid blocking the main UI thread, which could result in a poor user experience. You can use callbacks, threads, or libraries like AsyncTask or RxJava to handle asynchronous requests.

Permissions and Security

When making network requests, you may need to request permissions for internet access in your app's AndroidManifest.xml file:

```
<uses-permission android:name="android.permission.INTERNET" />
```

Additionally, consider security best practices, such as using HTTPS for secure communications and handling user data responsibly.

Conclusion

Making HTTP requests is a fundamental aspect of Android app development, enabling apps to interact with remote servers and APIs. Whether you choose to use HttpURLConnection or OkHttp, it's essential to handle network requests asynchronously and follow best practices for permissions and security to create a robust and secure app.

Section 8.2: Parsing JSON and XML

When working with network requests in Android, you often receive data in formats like JSON or XML. Parsing this data is a crucial step in extracting meaningful information that your app can use. In this section, we'll explore how to parse JSON and XML data in Android.

Parsing JSON

Using JSONObject

Android provides the `JSONObject` class to parse JSON data. Here's a basic example:

```
try {
    String json = "{\"name\":\"John\",\"age\":30,\"city\":\"New York\"}";
    JSONObject jsonObject = new JSONObject(json);

    String name = jsonObject.getString("name");
    int age = jsonObject.getInt("age");
    String city = jsonObject.getString("city");

    // Now you can use the parsed data
} catch (JSONException e) {
    e.printStackTrace();
}
```

Using Gson Library

The Gson library is a popular choice for parsing JSON in Android. To use Gson, include its dependency in your app's build.gradle file:

```
implementation 'com.google.code.gson:gson:2.8.8'
```

Here's an example of parsing JSON using Gson:

```
import com.google.gson.Gson;

// Define a class representing the JSON structure
class Person {
    String name;
    int age;
    String city;
}

// Parse JSON using Gson
String json = "{\"name\":\"John\",\"age\":30,\"city\":\"New York\"}";
Gson gson = new Gson();
Person person = gson.fromJson(json, Person.class);

// Now you can access the parsed data as person.name, person.age, etc.
```

Parsing XML

Using XmlPullParser

To parse XML data in Android, you can use the XmlPullParser class. It provides a streaming, pull-based approach to parse XML documents.

Here's a simplified example:

```java
try {
    String xml = "<person><name>John</name><age>30</age><city>New York</city>
</person>";
    XmlPullParserFactory factory = XmlPullParserFactory.newInstance();
    XmlPullParser parser = factory.newPullParser();
    parser.setInput(new StringReader(xml));

    int eventType = parser.getEventType();
    String name = "";
    int age = 0;
    String city = "";

    while (eventType != XmlPullParser.END_DOCUMENT) {
        String tagName = parser.getName();
        switch (eventType) {
            case XmlPullParser.START_TAG:
                break;
            case XmlPullParser.TEXT:
                if ("name".equals(tagName)) {
                    name = parser.getText();
                } else if ("age".equals(tagName)) {
                    age = Integer.parseInt(parser.getText());
                } else if ("city".equals(tagName)) {
                    city = parser.getText();
                }
                break;
            case XmlPullParser.END_TAG:
                break;
        }
        eventType = parser.next();
    }

    // Now you can use the parsed data
} catch (XmlPullParserException | IOException e) {
    e.printStackTrace();
}
```

Libraries for XML Parsing

If you need to work with more complex XML data, libraries like SimpleXML and XmlPullParser might be less convenient. Consider using libraries like JAXB or SimpleXML, which offer easier ways to map XML data to Java objects.

Conclusion

Parsing JSON and XML data is a common task when working with network requests in Android. Android provides built-in classes like `JSONObject` and `XmlPullParser` for basic parsing, but libraries like Gson can simplify the process for JSON. Depending on your project's complexity, you may choose different approaches and libraries to handle data parsing efficiently.

Section 8.3: Handling Network Permissions

When your Android app interacts with the internet, it must request specific permissions from the user to access network resources. This section discusses the importance of network permissions, how to request them, and best practices for handling them.

Importance of Network Permissions

Network permissions are essential because they determine an app's ability to access the internet and interact with remote servers, services, and APIs. Without these permissions, your app won't be able to make network requests, fetch data, or communicate with web services. This can severely limit your app's functionality.

Requesting Network Permissions

To request network permissions in your Android app, you need to declare them in the AndroidManifest.xml file. The following permission is the most commonly used one for internet access:

```
<uses-permission android:name="android.permission.INTERNET" />
```

This permission allows your app to establish network connections and access the internet. Without it, your app won't be able to send or receive data over the network.

Additional Permissions

In some cases, you may need more specific permissions depending on your app's requirements. Here are a few examples:

- `android.permission.ACCESS_NETWORK_STATE`: This permission allows your app to access information about the device's network state, such as whether it's connected to Wi-Fi or mobile data. It can be useful for optimizing data usage.

- `android.permission.ACCESS_WIFI_STATE`: This permission provides information about the device's Wi-Fi state, including whether Wi-Fi is enabled or disabled. It's useful for apps that need to interact with Wi-Fi networks.

- `android.permission.CHANGE_NETWORK_STATE` and `android.permission.CHANGE_WIFI_STATE`: These permissions allow your app to change network and Wi-Fi settings. They should be used with caution, as they can affect the user's device settings.

Best Practices

When handling network permissions in your Android app, consider the following best practices:

1. **Request Permissions at Runtime**: Starting from Android 6.0 (API level 23), users are prompted to grant permissions at runtime. Ensure that your app requests network permissions only when needed, and handle user denials gracefully.

2. **Check for Permissions**: Before performing network-related actions, check if the necessary permissions are granted. You can use the `PackageManager` to check permissions programmatically.

3. **Explain Why You Need Permissions**: When requesting permissions, provide a clear and concise explanation to users about why your app needs them. This improves user trust and understanding.

4. **Handle Permission Denials**: Your app should gracefully handle cases where users deny network permissions. Provide alternative functionality or explanations to users.

5. **Test on Devices with Different Network States**: Test your app on devices with different network states (e.g., Wi-Fi, mobile data, airplane mode) to ensure it behaves appropriately in various scenarios.

Conclusion

Network permissions are crucial for Android apps that require internet access. Requesting and handling these permissions properly is essential to ensure your app's functionality and maintain a positive user experience. Follow best practices to request permissions at runtime, explain the reasons for permission requests, and handle permission denials gracefully.

Section 8.4: Implementing RESTful APIs

REST (Representational State Transfer) is an architectural style used for designing networked applications. RESTful APIs (Application Programming Interfaces) follow this style and have become a standard for building web services that are easy to understand and use. In this section, we will explore how to implement RESTful APIs in Android apps.

RESTful APIs are based on a set of principles, including the following key concepts:

- **Resources**: Resources are the core abstractions in a RESTful API. They represent objects or data entities, such as users, products, or posts. Resources are identified by URLs.

- **HTTP Methods**: RESTful APIs use HTTP methods to perform actions on resources. Common HTTP methods include GET (retrieve data), POST (create data), PUT (update data), and DELETE (remove data).

- **Stateless**: Each API request from a client to a server must contain all the information needed to understand and fulfill the request. The server should not store any client state between requests.

- **Uniform Interface**: RESTful APIs provide a consistent and uniform way to interact with resources. This makes APIs easy to understand and use.

Making HTTP Requests

To interact with RESTful APIs in Android, you can use the `HttpURLConnection` class or popular third-party libraries like Retrofit or OkHttp. Here's a simplified example using `HttpURLConnection` to make a GET request:

```
try {
    // Create a URL object for the API endpoint
    URL url = new URL("https://api.example.com/resource");

    // Open a connection to the URL
    HttpURLConnection connection = (HttpURLConnection) url.openConnection();

    // Set the HTTP request method to GET
    connection.setRequestMethod("GET");

    // Read the response
    int responseCode = connection.getResponseCode();
    if (responseCode == HttpURLConnection.HTTP_OK) {
        // Read and process the response data
        BufferedReader reader = new BufferedReader(new InputStreamReader(connection.getInputStream()));
        String line;
        StringBuilder response = new StringBuilder();
        while ((line = reader.readLine()) != null) {
            response.append(line);
        }
        reader.close();
```

```
        // Process the JSON or XML response as needed
        String responseData = response.toString();
        // Handle the data...
    } else {
        // Handle the error response...
    }

    // Disconnect the connection
    connection.disconnect();
} catch (IOException e) {
    e.printStackTrace();
}
```

Using Retrofit

Retrofit is a popular library for making HTTP requests in Android. It simplifies the process of working with RESTful APIs by providing a high-level, declarative interface. Here's a basic example of how to use Retrofit:

```
// Define an interface with API endpoints
interface ApiService {
    @GET("resource")
    Call<ResponseBody> getResourceData();
}

// Create a Retrofit instance
Retrofit retrofit = new Retrofit.Builder()
    .baseUrl("https://api.example.com/")
    .addConverterFactory(GsonConverterFactory.create())
    .build();

// Create an instance of the API service
ApiService apiService = retrofit.create(ApiService.class);

// Make a GET request
Call<ResponseBody> call = apiService.getResourceData();
call.enqueue(new Callback<ResponseBody>() {
    @Override
    public void onResponse(Call<ResponseBody> call, Response<ResponseBody> re
sponse) {
        if (response.isSuccessful()) {
            // Handle the successful response here
        } else {
            // Handle the error response here
        }
    }

    @Override
    public void onFailure(Call<ResponseBody> call, Throwable t) {
```

```
            // Handle network failures here
    }
});
```

Many RESTful APIs require authentication for security purposes. You can include authentication headers or tokens in your HTTP requests. Depending on the API, this may involve using OAuth tokens, API keys, or other authentication mechanisms.

Conclusion

Implementing RESTful APIs in Android is a common task when building apps that interact with web services. Understanding the principles of REST, making HTTP requests, and using libraries like Retrofit can streamline the process. Always refer to the API documentation for specific details on how to authenticate and use the API endpoints effectively.

Section 8.5: Caching and Offline Access

Caching and offline access are important aspects of mobile app development, especially when dealing with networked data. They enhance the user experience by reducing data usage and providing content even when the device is offline. In this section, we'll explore caching strategies and techniques for enabling offline access in Android apps.

Caching Strategies

Caching involves storing previously fetched data locally on the device so that it can be quickly retrieved without making redundant network requests. Android provides several mechanisms for caching data:

1. **Memory Caching**: Android's LruCache class allows you to cache data in memory. This is suitable for small, frequently used data that can be easily recreated if purged from memory.

2. **Disk Caching**: For larger or persistent data, consider caching to disk. Popular libraries like Glide and Picasso offer disk caching for images. You can also implement your custom disk caching using the file system.

3. **HTTP Caching**: HTTP headers like Cache-Control and Expires can be used to control caching on the client and server sides. Android's HttpURLConnection supports caching by default. Retrofit and OkHttp also provide caching mechanisms.

Enabling Offline Access

Offline access is crucial for maintaining app functionality when the device is not connected to the internet. Here are some strategies for enabling offline access:

1. **Local Database**: Store essential data in a local database (e.g., SQLite) that can be accessed without an internet connection. This approach is common for apps that require access to content, such as news articles or user data, even when offline.

2. **Data Syncing**: Implement a synchronization mechanism that periodically updates local data with remote data when the device is online. This ensures that the local database is up-to-date, allowing users to interact with content offline.

3. **Offline-First Architecture**: Design your app with an "offline-first" approach, where the app functions as expected offline and syncs data when a network connection is available. This approach is useful for apps that need to work seamlessly regardless of connectivity.

4. **Caching Web Content**: For apps that display web content, consider caching web pages or content locally so that users can access it without an internet connection. WebView can be used to display cached web content.

Example of Simple Data Caching

Here's a simplified example of caching data using Android's LruCache:

```
import android.util.LruCache;

// Initialize an LruCache with a max size (in bytes)
LruCache<String, String> cache = new LruCache<>(1024 * 1024); // 1MB

// Store data in the cache
cache.put("key", "value");

// Retrieve data from the cache
String cachedValue = cache.get("key");
if (cachedValue != null) {
    // Use the cached data
} else {
    // Data is not in the cache; fetch it from the network or another source
}
```

Conclusion

Caching and enabling offline access are essential strategies for optimizing the performance and usability of Android apps. Depending on your app's requirements, you can implement different caching strategies and synchronization mechanisms to ensure that users have a seamless experience, even when they are not connected to the internet. These strategies help reduce data usage, improve app responsiveness, and enhance the overall user experience.

Chapter 9: Multimedia and Camera Integration

Section 9.1: Working with Images and Drawables

Working with images and drawables is a common task in Android app development. Whether you want to display images in your app's user interface, use them as icons, or manipulate them in various ways, Android provides a robust set of tools and libraries to help you work with images effectively.

Displaying Images

To display images in your app's user interface, you can use the `ImageView` widget. You can set the image source programmatically or through XML layout files. Here's an example of how to display an image in an `ImageView`:

```
<ImageView
    android:id="@+id/imageView"
    android:layout_width="wrap_content"
    android:layout_height="wrap_content"
    android:src="@drawable/my_image" />
```

In this example, `my_image` refers to the image resource located in the `res/drawable` directory of your Android project.

Loading Images Efficiently

Loading images efficiently is crucial to maintain app performance. If you're working with large images, consider using libraries like Glide or Picasso, which handle image loading, caching, and resizing automatically. Here's an example of how to load an image using Glide:

```
ImageView imageView = findViewById(R.id.imageView);
String imageUrl = "https://example.com/image.jpg";

Glide.with(this)
    .load(imageUrl)
    .placeholder(R.drawable.placeholder_image)
    .error(R.drawable.error_image)
    .into(imageView);
```

Glide will handle the background loading of the image, display a placeholder while loading, and show an error image if the load fails.

Working with Drawables

Android provides various drawable resources, including vector drawables, bitmap drawables, and shape drawables. Vector drawables are scalable and resolution-independent, making them a good choice for icons and graphics that need to adapt to different screen sizes and densities.

You can create vector drawables using tools like Android Studio's Vector Asset Studio or by defining them in XML. Here's an example of a vector drawable in XML:

```xml
<vector xmlns:android="http://schemas.android.com/apk/res/android"
    android:width="24dp"
    android:height="24dp"
    android:viewportWidth="24.0"
    android:viewportHeight="24.0">
    <path
        android:fillColor="#FF000000"
        android:pathData="M12,2C6.48,2 2,6.48 2,12s4.48,10 10,10s10,-4.48 10,
    -10S17.52,2 12,2zM11,17h-2v-2h2v2zm0,-4h-2V7h2v6z"/>
</vector>
```

Image Manipulation

If your app needs to manipulate images, you can use the Android Graphics and Bitmap classes to perform tasks like resizing, cropping, or applying filters. Here's an example of resizing a bitmap:

```java
Bitmap originalBitmap = BitmapFactory.decodeResource(getResources(), R.drawable.my_image);
int newWidth = 200;
int newHeight = 200;
Bitmap resizedBitmap = Bitmap.createScaledBitmap(originalBitmap, newWidth, newHeight, true);
```

Conclusion

Working with images and drawables is an essential part of Android app development. Whether you're displaying images in your app's user interface or performing more complex image manipulations, Android provides the tools and libraries to help you achieve your goals efficiently. Consider the performance implications when working with images, and use libraries like Glide or Picasso for image loading and caching to maintain a responsive user experience.

Section 9.2: Playing Audio and Video

In Android app development, playing audio and video is a common requirement for various types of apps, from media players to educational platforms. Android provides powerful features and APIs to work with audio and video playback, making it possible to create engaging multimedia experiences.

Playing Audio

To play audio in your Android app, you can use the MediaPlayer class or the more modern ExoPlayer library, which offers more advanced features and better support for streaming media. Here, we'll focus on MediaPlayer.

Using MediaPlayer
```
// Initialize MediaPlayer
MediaPlayer mediaPlayer = MediaPlayer.create(this, R.raw.audio_file);

// Start playback
mediaPlayer.start();

// Pause playback
mediaPlayer.pause();

// Release resources when done
mediaPlayer.release();
```

In this example, `R.raw.audio_file` refers to an audio resource located in the `res/raw` directory of your Android project. You can replace it with the path to your audio file.

Playing Video

Playing video in Android apps can be achieved using the `VideoView` widget or a more advanced player like `ExoPlayer`. Here, we'll use `VideoView` for simplicity.

Using VideoView
```
<VideoView
    android:id="@+id/videoView"
    android:layout_width="match_parent"
    android:layout_height="match_parent" />

// Initialize VideoView
VideoView videoView = findViewById(R.id.videoView);

// Set the video path
String videoPath = "android.resource://" + getPackageName() + "/" + R.raw.video_file;
videoView.setVideoURI(Uri.parse(videoPath));

// Start video playback
videoView.start();

// Pause video playback
videoView.pause();

// Stop video playback
videoView.stopPlayback();
```

In this example, `R.raw.video_file` refers to a video resource located in the `res/raw` directory of your Android project.

Streaming Media

For streaming audio and video from remote sources, consider using the `ExoPlayer` library, which provides support for adaptive streaming formats like HLS and DASH.

Audio and Video Recording

If your app needs to record audio or video, Android provides APIs for that as well. You can use the `MediaRecorder` class to capture audio and video from the device's microphone and camera.

Permissions

When working with audio and video, don't forget to request the necessary permissions from the user, such as the `RECORD_AUDIO`, `CAMERA`, and `INTERNET` permissions, depending on your app's functionality.

Conclusion

Playing audio and video is a fundamental part of many Android apps. Whether you're creating a music player, a video streaming app, or simply adding multimedia elements to your user interface, Android offers a range of tools and libraries to help you achieve your goals. Consider the specific requirements of your app, such as streaming, recording, or offline playback, and choose the appropriate APIs and libraries to create a seamless multimedia experience for your users.

Section 9.3: Recording Audio and Video

Recording audio and video is a common feature in many Android applications, from voice memo apps to video recording and sharing platforms. Android provides APIs to capture audio and video from device microphones and cameras, making it possible to add this functionality to your app.

Recording Audio

To record audio in your Android app, you can use the `MediaRecorder` class, which provides a straightforward way to capture audio from the device's microphone.

Using MediaRecorder for Audio Recording

Here's an example of how to set up and use `MediaRecorder` for audio recording:

```
// Initialize MediaRecorder
MediaRecorder mediaRecorder = new MediaRecorder();

// Set the audio source (microphone)
mediaRecorder.setAudioSource(MediaRecorder.AudioSource.MIC);
```

```java
// Set the output format and encoder
mediaRecorder.setOutputFormat(MediaRecorder.OutputFormat.MPEG_4);
mediaRecorder.setAudioEncoder(MediaRecorder.AudioEncoder.AAC);

// Set the output file path
String outputPath = getExternalFilesDir(Environment.DIRECTORY_MUSIC) + "/reco
rded_audio.mp4";
mediaRecorder.setOutputFile(outputPath);

// Prepare and start recording
try {
    mediaRecorder.prepare();
    mediaRecorder.start();
} catch (IOException e) {
    e.printStackTrace();
}

// Stop recording
mediaRecorder.stop();
mediaRecorder.reset();

// Release resources
mediaRecorder.release();
```

In this example, we set the audio source to the device's microphone, specify the output format and encoder, set the output file path, and then prepare and start the recording. After recording, we stop the `MediaRecorder`, reset it, and release its resources.

Recording Video

Recording video in Android apps can be achieved using the `MediaRecorder` class in combination with the device's camera.

Using MediaRecorder for Video Recording

Here's an example of how to set up and use `MediaRecorder` for video recording:

```java
// Initialize MediaRecorder
MediaRecorder mediaRecorder = new MediaRecorder();

// Set the video source (camera)
mediaRecorder.setVideoSource(MediaRecorder.VideoSource.CAMERA);

// Set the audio source (microphone)
mediaRecorder.setAudioSource(MediaRecorder.AudioSource.MIC);

// Set the output format and encoder
mediaRecorder.setOutputFormat(MediaRecorder.OutputFormat.MPEG_4);
mediaRecorder.setVideoEncoder(MediaRecorder.VideoEncoder.H264);
mediaRecorder.setAudioEncoder(MediaRecorder.AudioEncoder.AAC);
```

```java
// Set the output file path
String outputPath = getExternalFilesDir(Environment.DIRECTORY_MOVIES) + "/rec
orded_video.mp4";
mediaRecorder.setOutputFile(outputPath);

// Set the video size and frame rate
mediaRecorder.setVideoSize(1280, 720);
mediaRecorder.setVideoFrameRate(30);

// Prepare and start recording
try {
    mediaRecorder.prepare();
    mediaRecorder.start();
} catch (IOException e) {
    e.printStackTrace();
}

// Stop recording
mediaRecorder.stop();
mediaRecorder.reset();

// Release resources
mediaRecorder.release();
```

In this example, we set the video and audio sources to the device's camera and microphone, respectively, specify the output format and encoders, set the output file path, and configure video size and frame rate. Finally, we prepare and start the recording, stop it when done, reset the MediaRecorder, and release its resources.

Permissions

When working with audio and video recording, it's essential to request the necessary permissions from the user, such as the RECORD_AUDIO and CAMERA permissions, depending on your app's functionality.

Conclusion

Recording audio and video is a valuable feature for many Android applications. Whether you're creating a voice recording app, a video sharing platform, or any other app that involves capturing multimedia content, Android provides the tools and APIs to help you implement this functionality efficiently. Always remember to handle permissions and manage resources properly to ensure a smooth user experience.

Section 9.4: Integrating the Camera

Integrating the device's camera into your Android app opens up a wide range of possibilities, from capturing photos and videos to implementing augmented reality experiences. Android provides robust APIs for working with the camera, allowing you to create compelling visual features in your app.

Accessing the Camera

To access the camera in your Android app, you typically use the Camera2 API, which offers more advanced control and flexibility than the older Camera API. Here's an overview of how to use Camera2 for basic camera functionality.

```
Camera2 Basics
// Check for camera permissions
if (ContextCompat.checkSelfPermission(this, Manifest.permission.CAMERA) != Pa
ckageManager.PERMISSION_GRANTED) {
    // Request camera permission
    ActivityCompat.requestPermissions(this, new String[]{Manifest.permission.
CAMERA}, CAMERA_PERMISSION_REQUEST);
    return;
}

// Initialize CameraManager
CameraManager cameraManager = (CameraManager) getSystemService(Context.CAMERA
_SERVICE);

try {
    // Get the list of available cameras
    String[] cameraIds = cameraManager.getCameraIdList();

    // Open the first (rear) camera
    String cameraId = cameraIds[0];
    cameraManager.openCamera(cameraId, new CameraDevice.StateCallback() {
        @Override
        public void onOpened(@NonNull CameraDevice camera) {
            // Camera is ready for use, configure and start preview
            configureCameraAndStartPreview(camera);
        }

        @Override
        public void onDisconnected(@NonNull CameraDevice camera) {
            // Camera is disconnected
        }

        @Override
        public void onError(@NonNull CameraDevice camera, int error) {
```

```
                // Error occurred while opening the camera
            }
        }, null);
    } catch (CameraAccessException e) {
        e.printStackTrace();
    }
```

In this code snippet, we first check for camera permissions and request them if necessary. Then, we initialize the `CameraManager` to manage camera devices. We get the list of available camera IDs and open the first (usually rear) camera. The `CameraDevice.StateCallback` provides callbacks for camera state changes.

Capturing Photos

Capturing photos is a common camera-related task. To capture a photo using Camera2, you can use the following code as part of the `configureCameraAndStartPreview` method:

```
// Create a CameraCaptureSession
List<Surface> outputSurfaces = new ArrayList<>();
outputSurfaces.add(surfaceForPreview); // Surface for preview
outputSurfaces.add(imageReader.getSurface()); // Surface for capturing images

cameraDevice.createCaptureSession(outputSurfaces, new CameraCaptureSession.St
ateCallback() {
    @Override
    public void onConfigured(@NonNull CameraCaptureSession session) {
        try {
            // Create a CaptureRequest for image capture
            CaptureRequest.Builder captureBuilder = cameraDevice.createCaptur
eRequest(CameraDevice.TEMPLATE_STILL_CAPTURE);
            captureBuilder.addTarget(imageReader.getSurface());

            // Capture image
            session.capture(captureBuilder.build(), null, null);
        } catch (CameraAccessException e) {
            e.printStackTrace();
        }
    }

    @Override
    public void onConfigureFailed(@NonNull CameraCaptureSession session) {
        // Configuration failed
    }
}, null);
```

In this code, we create a `CameraCaptureSession` that includes a surface for the camera preview and a surface for capturing images (using an `ImageReader`). We then create a `CaptureRequest` for still capture and capture the image when the session is configured.

Recording Videos

Recording videos with Camera2 involves configuring media recording surfaces and creating a `MediaRecorder`. Here's a simplified example:

```
// Create a MediaRecorder
mediaRecorder = new MediaRecorder();
mediaRecorder.setVideoSource(MediaRecorder.VideoSource.SURFACE);
mediaRecorder.setAudioSource(MediaRecorder.AudioSource.MIC);
mediaRecorder.setOutputFormat(MediaRecorder.OutputFormat.MPEG_4);
mediaRecorder.setVideoEncoder(MediaRecorder.VideoEncoder.H264);
mediaRecorder.setAudioEncoder(MediaRecorder.AudioEncoder.AAC);
mediaRecorder.setOutputFile(outputVideoFile);

// Prepare and start recording
try {
    mediaRecorder.prepare();
    mediaRecorder.start();
} catch (IOException e) {
    e.printStackTrace();
}
```

In this code, we configure the `MediaRecorder` to use the camera's surface as the video source and the device's microphone as the audio source. We specify the output format and encoders, set the output file path, and start recording.

Augmented Reality (AR)

For more advanced camera applications, such as augmented reality (AR), you can use AR libraries like ARCore or ARKit (for iOS). These libraries provide tools for motion tracking, environmental understanding, and real-time 3D rendering, allowing you to create immersive AR experiences.

Conclusion

Integrating the camera into your Android app opens up opportunities for various features, including photo and video capture, AR, and more. The Camera2 API provides powerful tools for managing camera devices and capturing high-quality media content. However, keep in mind that camera functionality often requires careful handling of permissions, device compatibility, and resource management to provide a seamless user experience.

Section 9.5: Image Processing and Editing

Image processing and editing are essential aspects of many Android apps, from photo editors to social media platforms. This section explores techniques and libraries for performing image manipulation within your Android applications.

Basic Image Processing

Android provides the `Bitmap` class, which allows you to load, manipulate, and display images easily. Here are some common image processing tasks you can perform:

Loading an Image

```
Bitmap bitmap = BitmapFactory.decodeResource(getResources(), R.drawable.image
);
```

This code loads an image from a resource into a `Bitmap` object.

Resizing an Image

```
int newWidth = 300;
int newHeight = 200;
Bitmap resizedBitmap = Bitmap.createScaledBitmap(bitmap, newWidth, newHeight,
true);
```

Resizing a `Bitmap` involves creating a new `Bitmap` with the desired dimensions.

Rotating an Image

```
Matrix matrix = new Matrix();
matrix.postRotate(90); // Rotate by 90 degrees
Bitmap rotatedBitmap = Bitmap.createBitmap(bitmap, 0, 0, bitmap.getWidth(), b
itmap.getHeight(), matrix, true);
```

You can rotate a `Bitmap` by specifying the rotation angle and creating a new rotated `Bitmap`.

Advanced Image Processing

For more advanced image processing tasks like applying filters, enhancing colors, or implementing complex effects, you might want to consider using image processing libraries. A popular library for this purpose is OpenCV for Android.

Using OpenCV for Android

OpenCV (Open Source Computer Vision Library) provides a wide range of tools for image processing and computer vision tasks. To integrate OpenCV into your Android project, follow these steps:

1. Add the OpenCV Android Library to your project.
2. Initialize OpenCV in your app's main activity:

```
if (!OpenCVLoader.initDebug()) {
    Log.e(TAG, "OpenCV initialization failed.");
} else {
    Log.d(TAG, "OpenCV initialization succeeded.");
}
```

3. Use OpenCV functions to perform image processing tasks. For example, to apply a Gaussian blur:

```
Mat srcImage = Imgcodecs.imread(imagePath);
Mat blurredImage = new Mat();
Imgproc.GaussianBlur(srcImage, blurredImage, new Size(5, 5), 0);
```

Implementing an Image Editor

If you're building an image editing app, you'll need to implement features like cropping, adding text, applying filters, and more. This often involves creating a custom user interface and integrating image processing libraries as needed.

Building a Custom Image Editor

A custom image editor can be built using Android's UI components (e.g., `ImageView`, `SeekBar`, and `Canvas`) along with image processing libraries like OpenCV or GPUImage. You'll need to handle user interactions, such as selecting an editing tool, adjusting parameters, and previewing changes in real-time.

Conclusion

Image processing and editing are versatile capabilities that can enhance the functionality and user experience of your Android app. Whether you're applying basic transformations or implementing advanced image effects, Android provides the tools and libraries needed to create compelling visual experiences. Depending on your app's requirements, you can choose the appropriate techniques and libraries to achieve your image processing goals.

Chapter 10: Location-Based Services and Maps

Section 10.1: Getting Device Location

Location-based services are an integral part of many Android apps, enabling features such as mapping, geofencing, location tracking, and more. In this section, we'll explore how to retrieve the device's current location in your Android application.

Location Providers

Android provides several location providers to determine the device's location:

1. **GPS (Global Positioning System):** Provides highly accurate location information but requires an open sky view and can drain the device's battery quickly.

2. **Network Provider:** Uses Wi-Fi and cellular data to estimate the device's location. It's less accurate than GPS but works well in urban areas.

3. **Passive Provider:** Listens to location updates generated by other apps or providers. It doesn't actively request location updates but can be useful for conserving battery.

Requesting Location Updates

To obtain the device's location, you typically use the Fused Location Provider, which combines data from multiple sources to provide accurate and efficient location updates.

1. Add Permissions to Your Manifest

```
<uses-permission android:name="android.permission.ACCESS_FINE_LOCATION" />
<uses-permission android:name="android.permission.ACCESS_COARSE_LOCATION" />
```

Make sure to request these permissions in your AndroidManifest.xml.

2. Check and Request Permissions at Runtime

In Android 6.0 (API level 23) and higher, you must request location permissions at runtime if the user hasn't granted them yet. Here's how you can check and request permissions:

```
// Check if permission is granted
if (ContextCompat.checkSelfPermission(this, Manifest.permission.ACCESS_FINE_L
OCATION) == PackageManager.PERMISSION_GRANTED) {
    // Permission granted
} else {
    // Request permission
    ActivityCompat.requestPermissions(this, new String[]{Manifest.permission.
ACCESS_FINE_LOCATION}, REQUEST_LOCATION_PERMISSION);
}
```

```
LocationRequest locationRequest = LocationRequest.create()
    .setInterval(5000) // Request location updates every 5 seconds
    .setFastestInterval(2000) // Receive updates at least every 2 seconds
    .setPriority(LocationRequest.PRIORITY_HIGH_ACCURACY); // Use high accurac
y for GPS
```

4. Set Up Location Callbacks

To receive location updates, you need to create a callback using the FusedLocationProviderClient. Here's a basic example:

```
FusedLocationProviderClient fusedLocationClient = LocationServices.getFusedLo
cationProviderClient(this);

fusedLocationClient.requestLocationUpdates(locationRequest, locationCallback,
Looper.getMainLooper());
```

5. Handle Location Updates

```
LocationCallback locationCallback = new LocationCallback() {
    @Override
    public void onLocationResult(LocationResult locationResult) {
        if (locationResult != null) {
            Location location = locationResult.getLastLocation();
            // Handle the location update here
        }
    }
};
```

Conclusion

Retrieving the device's location is a fundamental task in location-based Android apps. By following the steps outlined in this section, you can request and receive location updates, allowing you to create apps that utilize location data for various purposes, such as mapping, navigation, and location-based notifications.

Section 10.2: Using Location Services

Location services in Android allow you to access a wide range of location-related information, including the user's current location, geofencing, and location history. In this section, we'll explore how to use location services effectively in your Android app.

Location Services Overview

Android provides the following key components for working with location services:

1. **Location Manager:** The LocationManager class is a system service that provides access to the device's location-related features. It allows you to request location updates from different providers (e.g., GPS, network, passive).

2. **Google Play Services:** Google Play Services offers the Fused Location Provider, which is a high-level location API that combines data from various sources to provide accurate and efficient location updates. It's the recommended way to access location information.

Requesting Location Updates with Fused Location Provider

To request location updates using the Fused Location Provider, follow these steps:

1. Set Up Google Play Services

Ensure that Google Play Services is available on the user's device and that you've included the necessary dependencies in your app's build.gradle file.

```
implementation 'com.google.android.gms:play-services-location:18.0.0'
```

2. Initialize Fused Location Provider
```
private FusedLocationProviderClient fusedLocationClient;

fusedLocationClient = LocationServices.getFusedLocationProviderClient(this);
```

3. Request Location Updates
```
LocationRequest locationRequest = LocationRequest.create()
    .setInterval(5000) // Request location updates every 5 seconds
    .setFastestInterval(2000) // Receive updates at least every 2 seconds
    .setPriority(LocationRequest.PRIORITY_HIGH_ACCURACY); // Use high accuracy for GPS

fusedLocationClient.requestLocationUpdates(locationRequest, locationCallback, Looper.getMainLooper());
```

4. Handle Location Updates
```
LocationCallback locationCallback = new LocationCallback() {
    @Override
    public void onLocationResult(LocationResult locationResult) {
        if (locationResult != null) {
            Location location = locationResult.getLastLocation();
            // Handle the location update here
        }
    }
};
```

Geofencing

Geofencing is a location-based feature that allows you to define virtual geographic boundaries and trigger actions when a device enters or exits these boundaries. You can use the `GeofencingClient` provided by Google Play Services to create and monitor geofences.

Location Permissions

Don't forget to request location permissions from the user at runtime if your app targets Android 6.0 (API level 23) or higher. Check and request permissions as demonstrated in Section 10.1.

Conclusion

Location services play a crucial role in many Android apps, from navigation and mapping applications to location-based marketing. By using the Fused Location Provider and following best practices for requesting and handling location updates, you can provide users with accurate and efficient location-related features in your app. Additionally, geofencing offers opportunities for creating location-aware experiences and triggering actions based on the user's physical location.

Section 10.3: Implementing Maps and Geocoding

Maps and geocoding are essential components of many location-based Android apps. Maps allow you to display geographic data visually, while geocoding enables you to convert between addresses and geographic coordinates. In this section, we'll explore how to implement maps and geocoding in your Android application.

Integrating Google Maps

To integrate Google Maps into your Android app, follow these steps:

1. **Enable the Google Maps API:** You need to enable the "Google Maps Android API" for your project on the Google Cloud Console. Obtain an API key that your app will use to access the maps service.

2. **Add the Google Maps SDK to Your App:** Add the Google Maps SDK to your app's build.gradle file.

   ```
   implementation 'com.google.android.gms:play-services-maps:18.0.0'
   ```

3. **Add the Map Fragment to Your Layout:** In your XML layout file, add a `MapFragment` or `SupportMapFragment` where you want the map to appear.

   ```
   <fragment
       android:id="@+id/map"
       android:name="com.google.android.gms.maps.SupportMapFragment"
   ```

```
        android:layout_width="match_parent"
        android:layout_height="match_parent" />
```

4. **Initialize the Map in Your Activity:** In your activity's onCreate method, initialize the map by obtaining a reference to the GoogleMap object.

```
SupportMapFragment mapFragment = (SupportMapFragment) getSupportFragmen
tManager()
        .findFragmentById(R.id.map);

mapFragment.getMapAsync(new OnMapReadyCallback() {
    @Override
    public void onMapReady(GoogleMap googleMap) {
        // You can now work with the GoogleMap object
    }
});
```

5. **Configure the Map:** Customize the map by adding markers, overlays, and other features as needed.

Geocoding and Reverse Geocoding

Geocoding is the process of converting an address (like "1600 Amphitheatre Parkway, Mountain View, CA") into geographic coordinates (latitude and longitude). Reverse geocoding, on the other hand, involves converting coordinates into a readable address.

To perform geocoding and reverse geocoding in Android, you can use the Geocoder class provided by the Android framework. Here's an example of how to perform geocoding:

```
Geocoder geocoder = new Geocoder(this);
List<Address> addresses = geocoder.getFromLocationName("1600 Amphitheatre Par
kway, Mountain View, CA", 1);

if (!addresses.isEmpty()) {
    Address address = addresses.get(0);
    double latitude = address.getLatitude();
    double longitude = address.getLongitude();
}
```

And here's an example of reverse geocoding:

```
Geocoder geocoder = new Geocoder(this);
List<Address> addresses = geocoder.getFromLocation(latitude, longitude, 1);

if (!addresses.isEmpty()) {
    Address address = addresses.get(0);
    String fullAddress = address.getAddressLine(0);
}
```

Remember that you need to request location permissions from the user to access their current location and perform geocoding or reverse geocoding. Check and request permissions as explained in Section 10.1.

Conclusion

Maps and geocoding are powerful tools for creating location-aware Android apps. By integrating Google Maps and using the `Geocoder` class, you can provide users with features such as displaying maps, adding markers, and converting between addresses and coordinates. Properly handling permissions is crucial to ensure that your app can access location data when needed.

Section 10.4: Location-Based Notifications

Location-based notifications are a powerful feature in Android apps that allow you to send notifications to users when they enter or exit specific geographical areas. These notifications can enhance user engagement and provide context-aware information. In this section, we'll explore how to implement location-based notifications in your Android app.

Geofencing

Geofencing is the core technology behind location-based notifications. It allows you to define geographical areas (geofences) and monitor when a device enters or exits these areas. To implement geofencing in your app, follow these steps:

1. **Set Up Google Play Services:** Ensure that you have Google Play Services integrated into your app. You can do this by adding the following dependency to your app's build.gradle file:

```
implementation 'com.google.android.gms:play-services-location:18.0.0'
```

2. **Create a Geofence:** Define the geofences you want to monitor by specifying their geographical coordinates, radius, and other parameters. You can create multiple geofences if needed.

```
Geofence geofence = new Geofence.Builder()
    .setRequestId("unique_geofence_id")
    .setCircularRegion(latitude, longitude, radius)
    .setExpirationDuration(Geofence.NEVER_EXPIRE)
    .setTransitionTypes(Geofence.GEOFENCE_ENTER | Geofence.GEOFENCE_EXI
T)
    .build();
```

3. **Create a Geofencing Request:** Bundle your geofences into a `GeofencingRequest` and specify the triggering behavior.

```java
GeofencingRequest geofencingRequest = new GeofencingRequest.Builder()
    .setInitialTrigger(GeofencingRequest.INITIAL_TRIGGER_ENTER)
    .addGeofence(geofence)
    .build();
```

4. **Request Geofence Updates:** Request geofence updates by creating a PendingIntent that will be triggered when a geofence event occurs.

```java
PendingIntent geofencePendingIntent = PendingIntent.getService(
    this,
    0,
    new Intent(this, GeofenceService.class),
    PendingIntent.FLAG_UPDATE_CURRENT
);

if (ActivityCompat.checkSelfPermission(this, Manifest.permission.ACCESS
_FINE_LOCATION) == PackageManager.PERMISSION_GRANTED) {
    geofencingClient.addGeofences(geofencingRequest, geofencePendingInt
ent)
        .addOnSuccessListener(new OnSuccessListener<Void>() {
            @Override
            public void onSuccess(Void aVoid) {
                // Geofences added successfully
            }
        })
        .addOnFailureListener(new OnFailureListener() {
            @Override
            public void onFailure(@NonNull Exception e) {
                // Handle failure
            }
        });
}
```

5. **Handle Geofence Events:** When a device enters or exits a geofence, the GeofenceService will be triggered, and you can handle the event accordingly.

```java
public class GeofenceService extends IntentService {
    @Override
    protected void onHandleIntent(Intent intent) {
        GeofencingEvent geofencingEvent = GeofencingEvent.fromIntent(in
tent);
        if (geofencingEvent.hasError()) {
            // Handle error
            return;
        }

        int transitionType = geofencingEvent.getGeofenceTransition();
        if (transitionType == Geofence.GEOFENCE_TRANSITION_ENTER) {
            // Device entered a geofence
            // Trigger a notification or perform other actions
```

```
        } else if (transitionType == Geofence.GEOFENCE_TRANSITION_EXIT)
    {
            // Device exited a geofence
            // Trigger a notification or perform other actions
        }
    }
}
```

Permissions

To use location-based notifications, you must request location permissions from the user as discussed in Section 10.1.

Conclusion

Location-based notifications powered by geofencing can greatly enhance the user experience of your Android app. By monitoring geographical areas and triggering notifications based on user location, you can provide context-aware information and engage users in a meaningful way. Properly handle permissions and geofence events to ensure the reliability and effectiveness of this feature.

Section 10.5: Building Location-Aware Apps

Building location-aware apps is a valuable capability in the Android ecosystem. Location awareness allows you to provide users with location-based services, enhance user experiences, and offer features like geolocation, location tracking, and mapping. In this section, we'll explore the key aspects of building location-aware Android apps.

Location Providers

Android provides various location providers to access device location information. The primary location providers include:

- **GPS Provider:** This provider uses the device's built-in GPS sensor to determine the precise location. It provides accurate location data but may require a clear view of the sky and can drain the device's battery.

- **Network Provider:** The network provider uses cell tower and Wi-Fi signals to estimate the device's location. It's faster than GPS but less accurate. It's a good choice for location-aware apps in urban areas.

- **Fused Location Provider:** Introduced in the Google Play services, the Fused Location Provider combines data from multiple sources (including GPS, network, and sensors) to provide the best location estimate. It balances accuracy and power efficiency.

Requesting Location Permissions

To access device location, your app must request the appropriate permissions from the user. You typically request the ACCESS_FINE_LOCATION or ACCESS_COARSE_LOCATION permission, depending on your app's needs. Here's how you can request location permissions:

```java
// Check if the app has location permissions
if (ContextCompat.checkSelfPermission(this, Manifest.permission.ACCESS_FINE_LOCATION)
        != PackageManager.PERMISSION_GRANTED) {
    // Request location permissions
    ActivityCompat.requestPermissions(this,
            new String[]{Manifest.permission.ACCESS_FINE_LOCATION},
            LOCATION_PERMISSION_REQUEST_CODE);
}
```

Location Updates

To receive location updates, you can use the LocationManager or the more modern FusedLocationProviderClient from Google Play services. Here's an example of how to request location updates using the FusedLocationProviderClient:

```java
// Create an instance of FusedLocationProviderClient
FusedLocationProviderClient client = LocationServices.getFusedLocationProviderClient(this);

// Request location updates
LocationRequest locationRequest = new LocationRequest()
        .setInterval(10000) // Update interval in milliseconds
        .setFastestInterval(5000) // Fastest update interval
        .setPriority(LocationRequest.PRIORITY_HIGH_ACCURACY); // Accuracy level

client.requestLocationUpdates(locationRequest, locationCallback, null);
```

Handling Location Changes

When location updates are received, you can handle them in a LocationCallback:

```java
LocationCallback locationCallback = new LocationCallback() {
    @Override
    public void onLocationResult(LocationResult locationResult) {
        super.onLocationResult(locationResult);
        if (locationResult != null) {
            Location location = locationResult.getLastLocation();
            // Handle the new location data
        }
    }
};
```

Location Services Settings

You can prompt users to enable location services if they are disabled. Use an `AlertDialog` to guide users to the settings screen:

```
AlertDialog.Builder builder = new AlertDialog.Builder(this);
builder.setMessage("Location services are disabled. Do you want to enable the
m?")
        .setPositiveButton("Yes", new DialogInterface.OnClickListener() {
            public void onClick(DialogInterface dialog, int id) {
                // Open location settings
                Intent intent = new Intent(Settings.ACTION_LOCATION_SOURCE_SE
TTINGS);
                startActivity(intent);
            }
        })
        .setNegativeButton("No", new DialogInterface.OnClickListener() {
            public void onClick(DialogInterface dialog, int id) {
                // User declined, handle accordingly
            }
        });
AlertDialog dialog = builder.create();
dialog.show();
```

Conclusion

Building location-aware Android apps can significantly enhance the user experience by providing context-aware services and features. Understanding the different location providers, requesting permissions, and efficiently handling location updates are key steps in creating successful location-aware apps. Always consider user privacy and battery optimization when designing your app's location features.

Chapter 11: Building User Authentication

Section 11.1: User Authentication Basics

User authentication is a fundamental aspect of many Android applications, especially those that require user-specific data or interaction. It ensures that users are who they claim to be before granting access to certain features or data. This section provides an overview of user authentication basics in Android app development.

Why User Authentication Matters

User authentication serves several critical purposes in mobile apps:

1. **User Identity Verification**: Authentication confirms the user's identity, preventing unauthorized access.

2. **Data Security**: It helps protect user data from unauthorized access or tampering.

3. **Personalization**: Authenticated users can have personalized experiences and access to their data.

4. **Authorization**: Authentication is often the first step in determining what features or data a user can access.

Common Authentication Methods

There are various methods to implement user authentication in Android apps:

1. Email/Password Authentication
- This method involves users creating an account with their email and a password.
- The app stores encrypted passwords and checks them during login.
- Firebase Authentication is a popular service for implementing this method.

2. Social Media Authentication
- Apps can allow users to log in using their social media accounts like Google, Facebook, or Twitter.
- OAuth2 or similar protocols are used for this type of authentication.

3. Biometric Authentication
- Android devices support biometric methods like fingerprint or face recognition.
- Apps can use the BiometricPrompt API for secure biometric authentication.

4. Single Sign-On (SSO)
- SSO allows users to log in once and access multiple services without re-entering credentials.
- It's commonly used for enterprise apps.

User authentication should be implemented securely to protect user data and privacy:

1. **Password Security**: If using passwords, store them securely using hashing and salting techniques.

2. **Token-Based Authentication**: Use tokens for session management to avoid exposing sensitive user data.

3. **OAuth2**: Implement OAuth2 correctly to protect user authorization tokens.

4. **Secure Communication**: Ensure secure transmission of authentication data over HTTPS.

User Profile Management

After authentication, apps often manage user profiles, which may include personal information, settings, and preferences. Profile management is an essential part of user authentication systems.

In the upcoming sections, we'll delve deeper into implementing various authentication methods and best practices. Building a robust authentication system is crucial for the security and usability of your Android app.

Section 11.2: Implementing Email/Password Authentication

Implementing email/password authentication is a common approach for user sign-up and login in Android apps. This method allows users to create accounts with their email addresses and passwords. Firebase Authentication is a popular service that simplifies the implementation of email/password authentication. In this section, we'll explore the steps to implement this method.

Prerequisites

Before implementing email/password authentication, make sure you have the following set up:

1. **Firebase Project**: Create a Firebase project on the Firebase Console (https://console.firebase.google.com/).

2. **Firebase Android SDK**: Add the Firebase Android SDK to your app by adding the Firebase configuration file (`google-services.json`) and the necessary dependencies in your app-level `build.gradle` file.

Steps to Implement Email/Password Authentication

1. Set Up Firebase

- Add the Firebase Authentication SDK to your app-level `build.gradle`:

```
implementation 'com.google.firebase:firebase-auth:21.0.1'
```

- Initialize Firebase in your app's `onCreate` method:

```java
// Add this in your MainActivity.java or Application class
FirebaseApp.initializeApp(this);
```

2. Create a User Account

- To allow users to create accounts, you'll typically provide a registration form where they can enter their email and password.

- Use Firebase Authentication to create a new user account with the provided email and password:

```java
FirebaseAuth auth = FirebaseAuth.getInstance();

String email = "user@example.com";
String password = "password123";

auth.createUserWithEmailAndPassword(email, password)
    .addOnCompleteListener(this, task -> {
        if (task.isSuccessful()) {
            // Registration success
            FirebaseUser user = auth.getCurrentUser();
            // You can now store additional user information if needed.
        } else {
            // Registration failed
            Exception exception = task.getException();
            // Handle the error
        }
    });
```

3. User Login

- Implement user login with email and password using Firebase Authentication:

```java
FirebaseAuth auth = FirebaseAuth.getInstance();

String email = "user@example.com";
String password = "password123";

auth.signInWithEmailAndPassword(email, password)
    .addOnCompleteListener(this, task -> {
        if (task.isSuccessful()) {
            // Login success
            FirebaseUser user = auth.getCurrentUser();
```

```
            // You can now grant access to user-specific features.
        } else {
            // Login failed
            Exception exception = task.getException();
            // Handle the error

        }
    });
```

4. Sign Out

- Allow users to sign out when they choose to log out of your app:

```
FirebaseAuth auth = FirebaseAuth.getInstance();
auth.signOut();
```

Security Considerations

When implementing email/password authentication, it's essential to consider security best practices:

- **Password Storage**: Store user passwords securely using cryptographic hashing and salting techniques to protect against data breaches.

- **Account Recovery**: Implement account recovery mechanisms like email verification and password reset.

- **Rate Limiting**: Implement rate limiting and account lockout mechanisms to prevent brute-force attacks.

- **HTTPS**: Ensure that authentication requests are made over a secure HTTPS connection to protect user data during transmission.

By following these steps and security practices, you can implement robust email/password authentication in your Android app, providing a secure and user-friendly experience for your users.

Section 11.3: Social Media Authentication

In addition to email/password authentication, many Android apps offer the option for users to sign in or link their accounts with social media platforms such as Google, Facebook, Twitter, or GitHub. This allows for a streamlined and user-friendly login experience while leveraging the trust and security of established social media providers. In this section, we'll explore the implementation of social media authentication in Android apps.

Firebase Authentication simplifies the process of integrating social media authentication methods into your Android app. Here are the general steps to implement social media authentication using Firebase:

1. **Set Up Social Media Credentials**: To enable social media authentication, you must create developer accounts and obtain API credentials for each social media platform you want to support. This typically involves creating a project on the respective developer platform, registering your app, and obtaining API keys and secrets.

2. **Integrate Firebase Authentication**: Ensure you have Firebase Authentication set up in your Android app, as described in previous sections.

3. **Configure Social Media Providers**: In your Firebase project settings, configure the social media authentication providers you want to use (e.g., Google, Facebook, Twitter). You'll need to provide the API credentials obtained in step 1.

4. **Implement Sign-In Flow**: Create a user interface that allows users to choose their preferred social media provider for authentication. When the user selects a provider, trigger the Firebase authentication process for that provider.

5. **Handle Authentication Callbacks**: Firebase Authentication will handle the authentication process with the selected social media provider. You'll need to implement callback functions to handle the result of the authentication process.

Example: Google Sign-In

Here's a simplified example of how to implement Google Sign-In using Firebase Authentication:

```
// Initialize Firebase Authentication
FirebaseAuth auth = FirebaseAuth.getInstance();

// Configure Google Sign-In
GoogleSignInOptions gso = new GoogleSignInOptions.Builder(GoogleSignInOptions
.DEFAULT_SIGN_IN)
        .requestIdToken(getString(R.string.default_web_client_id))
        .requestEmail()
        .build();

GoogleSignInClient googleSignInClient = GoogleSignIn.getClient(this, gso);

// Implement Google Sign-In
void signInWithGoogle() {
    Intent signInIntent = googleSignInClient.getSignInIntent();
    startActivityForResult(signInIntent, RC_SIGN_IN);
}

// Handle the result of the Google Sign-In activity
```

```java
@Override
protected void onActivityResult(int requestCode, int resultCode, Intent data)
{
    super.onActivityResult(requestCode, resultCode, data);

    if (requestCode == RC_SIGN_IN) {
        Task<GoogleSignInAccount> task = GoogleSignIn.getSignedInAccountFromI
ntent(data);
        try {
            GoogleSignInAccount account = task.getResult(ApiException.class);
            if (account != null) {
                // Signed in successfully, authenticate with Firebase
                AuthCredential credential = GoogleAuthProvider.getCredential(
account.getIdToken(), null);
                auth.signInWithCredential(credential)
                        .addOnCompleteListener(this, task1 -> {
                            if (task1.isSuccessful()) {
                                // Authentication success
                                FirebaseUser user = auth.getCurrentUser();
                                // Update UI or perform other actions
                            } else {
                                // Authentication failed
                                // Handle the error
                            }
                        });
            }
        } catch (ApiException e) {
            // Google Sign-In failed
            // Handle the error
        }
    }
}
```

This example demonstrates the Google Sign-In process, but similar approaches apply to other social media providers. Firebase Authentication provides consistent methods for handling authentication across various platforms, making it a powerful tool for social media authentication in Android apps.

Security Considerations

When implementing social media authentication, consider the following security best practices:

- **Access Control**: Limit access to certain features or data based on the user's authentication status and user roles.

- **Account Linking**: Implement logic to handle cases where a user links their social media account with an existing email/password account.

- **Privacy Compliance**: Ensure that your app complies with privacy regulations, especially when dealing with user data from social media platforms.

- **Error Handling**: Implement robust error handling to gracefully handle authentication failures and edge cases.

By following these steps and best practices, you can implement social media authentication in your Android app, providing users with a convenient and secure login option.

Section 11.4: Security Considerations

Implementing user authentication, whether through email/password or social media, is a critical aspect of Android app development. However, with great power comes great responsibility, and ensuring the security of user authentication is of utmost importance. In this section, we'll delve into the security considerations you should keep in mind when implementing authentication in your Android app.

1. Protecting User Data

When users create accounts or log in to your app, they trust you with their personal information. It's essential to safeguard this data by employing encryption and secure communication protocols. Here are key security measures:

- **Use HTTPS**: Always transmit authentication data over HTTPS to encrypt the communication between the app and the server.

- **Data Encryption**: Store sensitive user data, such as passwords, securely by encrypting it. Avoid storing plaintext passwords.

- **Password Hashing**: Hash and salt user passwords before storing them in your database. Use robust hashing algorithms like bcrypt or scrypt.

2. Secure Authentication Tokens

Authentication tokens, like session tokens or JWTs (JSON Web Tokens), are used to verify the identity of users after they log in. Ensure their security:

- **JWT Security**: If using JWTs, sign them with a strong secret key and validate their signatures.

- **Short-Lived Tokens**: Use short-lived tokens to reduce the window of exposure if a token is compromised.

- **Token Storage**: Securely store tokens on the client side, preferably in the device's secure storage.

3. Account Recovery and Reset

Provide mechanisms for users to recover their accounts or reset their passwords while maintaining security:

- **Email Verification**: Require users to verify their email addresses to ensure the validity of their accounts.

- **Password Reset**: Implement a secure password reset mechanism that verifies the user's identity through email or other means.

4. Rate Limiting and Brute-Force Protection

To prevent brute-force attacks on login endpoints, implement rate limiting and account lockout policies:

- **Rate Limiting**: Limit the number of login attempts within a certain time frame.

- **Account Lockout**: Temporarily lock user accounts after a specified number of failed login attempts.

5. OAuth and OAuth 2.0

When implementing social media authentication using OAuth or OAuth 2.0, follow best practices:

- **OAuth Scope**: Only request the necessary permissions from users.

- **Token Security**: Keep OAuth tokens secure, as they can grant access to user data on social media platforms.

6. Third-Party Libraries

Be cautious when using third-party authentication libraries. Ensure that they are actively maintained and follow security best practices.

7. Session Management

Handle user sessions securely:

- **Session Expiry**: Set session timeouts and regularly validate sessions.

- **Logout**: Provide a secure logout mechanism to invalidate user sessions.

8. User Data Protection

Adhere to privacy regulations like GDPR and ensure that you protect user data according to these standards.

9. Continuous Monitoring

Regularly monitor your authentication system for vulnerabilities and security breaches. Implement logging and auditing to track login attempts and suspicious activities.

10. Education and Awareness

Educate your development team about security best practices and keep up-to-date with the latest security threats and solutions.

Incorporating these security considerations into your Android app's authentication system will help protect user data and maintain the trust of your user base. Remember that security is an ongoing process, and it's crucial to stay vigilant and proactive in identifying and addressing potential vulnerabilities.

Section 11.5: User Profile Management

User profile management is a crucial component of many Android applications, especially those that require user registration and authentication. It allows users to customize their experience, update their information, and control their account settings within the app. In this section, we'll explore best practices for implementing user profile management in your Android app.

1. User Registration and Profile Creation

When a user registers for your app, you'll typically collect some basic information to create their initial profile. This might include:

- **Username**: A unique identifier for the user.

- **Email**: The user's email address (used for communication and account recovery).

- **Password**: A secure, hashed password.

- **Profile Picture**: An optional user avatar or profile picture.

- **Additional Information**: Any other relevant user details, such as name, age, or location.

Ensure that your registration process is user-friendly and includes appropriate validation to prevent errors during sign-up.

2. Profile Editing and Updating

Allow users to edit and update their profiles. Common profile updates include changing the profile picture, updating contact information, and modifying personal details. Ensure that users can easily access the profile editing functionality within the app.

3. Password Change and Reset

Implement a secure mechanism for users to change their passwords. Additionally, provide a password reset feature that allows users to regain access to their accounts if they forget their passwords. This often involves sending a password reset link to the user's registered email address.

4. Account Deactivation and Deletion

Allow users to deactivate or delete their accounts if they wish to stop using your app. Make this process clear and accessible. Deactivation usually allows users to return later and reactivate their accounts, while account deletion permanently removes all user data.

5. Profile Privacy Settings

Some users may have privacy concerns and may want to control who can view their profile or specific information within it. Consider implementing privacy settings that allow users to choose who can see their profile details and what information is publicly visible.

6. User Preferences

Allow users to set preferences that customize their app experience. This might include notification settings, theme preferences, language preferences, or any other app-specific customization options.

7. Profile Verification

In some apps, especially those involving user interactions or transactions, consider implementing a profile verification system. This can involve verifying users' email addresses, phone numbers, or other identifying information to enhance trust within the community.

8. Data Privacy and Security

Maintain the highest standards of data privacy and security when handling user profile data. Encrypt sensitive information, use secure communication protocols, and regularly audit and test your security measures.

9. User Communication

Enable users to communicate with each other within the app if it's relevant to your application's functionality. Implement features such as messaging, chat, or commenting on posts or content.

10. User Feedback

Listen to user feedback regarding the profile management experience. Users may have suggestions for improvements or feature requests that can enhance their experience.

Remember that user profile management is an ongoing process, and it's essential to continuously improve and refine this aspect of your app based on user feedback and changing user needs. A well-designed and user-friendly profile management system can contribute significantly to user satisfaction and engagement with your Android app.

Chapter 12: Advanced App Navigation

Section 12.1: Navigation Components

Navigation is a critical aspect of Android app development, and it plays a significant role in ensuring a seamless and intuitive user experience. In this section, we'll explore the use of Navigation Components, a framework provided by Android Jetpack, to simplify and enhance app navigation.

What are Navigation Components?

Navigation Components are a set of libraries, tools, and plugins that help you implement navigation patterns in your Android app. They are part of the Android Jetpack library and offer several advantages:

1. **Simplified Navigation Graph**: Navigation Components use a visual editor in Android Studio, allowing you to create a navigation graph that represents the flow of your app. This graph makes it easy to visualize and manage the navigation paths between different screens or destinations in your app.

2. **Type-Safe Navigation**: Navigation Components provide type-safe navigation, reducing the risk of runtime errors related to incorrect destinations or arguments. You can specify the destination and argument types in XML, and the framework generates the necessary code for you.

3. **Back Stack Management**: Managing the back stack (the sequence of screens or fragments that the user has navigated through) is crucial for maintaining a coherent navigation experience. Navigation Components simplify this by handling the back stack automatically.

4. **Deep Linking**: Deep linking allows you to launch a specific screen in your app from an external link or URL. Navigation Components make it easy to set up deep linking for your app.

5. **Animation and Transition Support**: You can define custom animations and transitions between destinations, enhancing the visual appeal of your app's navigation.

Key Components of Navigation Components

Navigation Components consist of the following key components:

- **Navigation Graph**: This is an XML resource that defines the structure of your app's navigation. It specifies the destinations (screens or fragments) and the actions (transitions) between them.

- **NavHost**: A NavHost is a container in your layout where destinations are swapped in and out as the user navigates through your app. It is typically implemented as a FragmentContainerView or a FragmentContainer.

- **NavController**: NavController is responsible for handling navigation within your app. It manages the back stack and facilitates transitions between destinations.

- **NavDirection**: Directions are generated classes that represent possible navigation actions between destinations. They are type-safe and help ensure that you navigate to the correct destinations with the right arguments.

Using Navigation Components

To use Navigation Components in your Android app, follow these steps:

1. **Add Dependencies**: Add the Navigation library to your app's build.gradle file.

   ```
   implementation "androidx.navigation:navigation-fragment-ktx:2.4.0"
   implementation "androidx.navigation:navigation-ui-ktx:2.4.0"
   ```

2. **Create a Navigation Graph**: Create an XML navigation resource file that defines the navigation graph for your app. This file specifies the destinations and actions.

3. **Set Up a NavHost**: In your app's layout file, add a NavHost (typically a FragmentContainerView) where your destinations will be displayed.

4. **Associate NavHost with NavController**: In your activity or fragment, obtain a reference to the NavController and associate it with the NavHost.

5. **Navigate Between Destinations**: Use NavController to navigate between destinations using actions defined in the navigation graph.

6. **Handle Back Navigation**: Navigation Components automatically handle back navigation, but you can customize this behavior if needed.

7. **Deep Linking**: Implement deep linking if your app needs to handle external links.

Benefits of Navigation Components

Navigation Components offer several benefits, including:

- **Simplified Navigation Logic**: The framework simplifies the implementation of navigation logic, reducing boilerplate code.

- **Improved Code Organization**: With a clear visual representation of the navigation graph, your codebase becomes more organized and easier to maintain.

- **Type Safety**: Type-safe navigation prevents runtime errors and improves code quality.

- **Testability**: Navigation Components make it easier to write UI tests for navigation scenarios.

- **Flexibility**: While Navigation Components provide a robust default setup, you can customize navigation behavior to suit your app's specific requirements.

In the next sections, we'll delve deeper into various aspects of advanced app navigation, including deep links, navigation transitions, and multi-screen app development.

Section 12.2: Implementing Deep Links

Deep linking is a powerful feature in mobile app development that allows users to navigate directly to a specific screen within an app by clicking on a URL or a link. In Android, you can implement deep links using Navigation Components to provide a seamless and user-friendly experience.

What are Deep Links?

A deep link is a URL that points to a specific location within a mobile app, such as a particular screen or view. Deep links are used to seamlessly open an app and take the user directly to the content or feature they are interested in, bypassing the app's home screen. They are particularly useful for improving user engagement and providing a smoother user experience.

Deep links can be triggered from various sources, including web links, push notifications, SMS messages, or other apps. When a deep link is clicked, Android checks if the corresponding app is installed. If it is, the app is opened and directed to the specified location. If not, the user can be redirected to the app's download page on the Google Play Store.

Implementing Deep Links with Navigation Components

To implement deep links in your Android app using Navigation Components, follow these steps:

1. **Define Deep Link URIs**: Determine the URIs that will trigger deep links in your app. These URIs should correspond to specific destinations within your app.

2. **Configure the Navigation Graph**: In your navigation graph XML file, specify the deep link URIs for each destination using the `<deepLink>` element. You can also set additional attributes like the host and port.

```
<fragment
    android:id="@+id/deep_linked_destination"
    android:name="com.example.myapp.DeepLinkedDestinationFragment"
    android:label="Deep Linked Destination">
    <deepLink
        android:id="@+id/deep_link_uri"
```

```
            app:uri="exampleapp://deeplink" />
    </fragment>
```

3. **Handle Deep Links in the Activity**: In your app's main activity, configure deep link handling by overriding the onCreate method and using the AppLinks class to handle the deep link URI.

```
class MainActivity : AppCompatActivity() {
    override fun onCreate(savedInstanceState: Bundle?) {
        super.onCreate(savedInstanceState)
        setContentView(R.layout.activity_main)

        // Handle deep links
        val deepLinkUri = intent.data
        if (deepLinkUri != null) {
            val navController = findNavController(R.id.nav_host_fragmen
t)
            navController.handleDeepLink(deepLinkUri)
        }
    }
}
```

4. **Testing Deep Links**: To test deep links, you can use Android's ADB (Android Debug Bridge) tool. Run the following command to trigger a deep link:

```
adb shell am start -a android.intent.action.VIEW -d "exampleapp://deepl
ink"
```

5. **Testing on Emulators and Devices**: You can also test deep links on emulators and physical devices by clicking on links or using the adb command.

6. **Fallback URLs**: It's a good practice to specify fallback URLs in case the app is not installed on the user's device. You can do this by adding a data element with a web URL in your deep link configuration.

```
<deepLink
    android:id="@+id/deep_link_uri"
    app:uri="exampleapp://deeplink"
    android:autoVerify="true">
    <action android:name="android.intent.action.VIEW" />
    <category android:name="android.intent.category.DEFAULT" />
    <category android:name="android.intent.category.BROWSABLE" />
</deepLink>
<data android:scheme="http" android:host="example.com" />
```

By implementing deep links using Navigation Components, you enhance user engagement and provide a seamless transition from external sources to your app's specific content, improving the overall user experience.

In the next section, we'll explore how to handle navigation transitions effectively, creating a visually appealing app.

Section 12.3: Handling Navigation Transitions

Navigation transitions are an essential aspect of creating a visually appealing and user-friendly Android app. Smooth and well-designed transitions can significantly improve the user experience and make your app feel polished. In this section, we'll explore various techniques and tools to handle navigation transitions effectively.

Understanding Navigation Transitions

Navigation transitions refer to the animations and visual effects that occur when users move between different screens or fragments within your app. These transitions can include animations like slide-ins, fade-ins, or custom effects, making the navigation flow more intuitive and engaging.

Android provides several tools and libraries to help you create smooth navigation transitions:

1. **Navigation Components**: If you're using Navigation Components for app navigation (as discussed in previous sections), you can define custom animations between destinations in your navigation graph XML file. This allows you to specify how screens enter and exit the view.

```
<action
    android:id="@+id/action_to_destination"
    app:destination="@id/destination_fragment"
    app:enterAnim="@anim/slide_in_right"
    app:exitAnim="@anim/slide_out_left"
    app:popEnterAnim="@anim/slide_in_left"
    app:popExitAnim="@anim/slide_out_right" />
```

2. **Transition Framework**: Android's Transition framework allows you to create complex animations between views or fragments. You can define transitions like shared element transitions, fade transitions, and more.

```
val transition = TransitionInflater.from(context).inflateTransition(android.R.transition.fade)
fragment.sharedElementEnterTransition = transition
```

3. **MotionLayout**: MotionLayout is a powerful layout class that enables you to create complex animations and transitions by defining motion scenes. It's suitable for creating custom, interactive animations between views.

```
<MotionScene xmlns:app="http://schemas.android.com/apk/res-auto">
    <Transition
        app:constraintSetStart="@id/start"
```

```
        app:constraintSetEnd="@id/end">
        <OnSwipe
            app:touchAnchorId="@id/swipe_target"
            app:touchAnchorSide="bottom" />
    </Transition>
</MotionScene>
```

4. **Lottie**: Lottie is a library for rendering After Effects animations in real-time in Android apps. You can use Lottie to add delightful animations to your navigation transitions.

```
val animationView = findViewById<LottieAnimationView>(R.id.animation_vi
ew)
animationView.setAnimation("loading.json")
animationView.playAnimation()
```

Best Practices for Navigation Transitions

To create effective navigation transitions in your Android app, consider the following best practices:

1. **Keep It Simple**: Avoid overly complex animations that might confuse users. Focus on providing clear and straightforward transitions that enhance the user experience.

2. **Use Meaningful Animations**: Ensure that your animations have a purpose. They should help users understand the app's navigation flow or provide visual feedback.

3. **Consistency**: Maintain consistency in your navigation transitions throughout the app. Use similar animations for similar actions to create a coherent user experience.

4. **Performance**: Test your animations on various devices to ensure they perform well. Overly complex or resource-intensive animations can negatively impact app performance.

5. **User Feedback**: Consider providing feedback animations for user actions, such as button presses or form submissions. These animations can confirm to users that their actions were successful.

6. **Testing**: Thoroughly test your navigation transitions on different devices and screen sizes to ensure they work as expected in various scenarios.

By implementing well-designed navigation transitions, you can enhance your Android app's overall user experience and make it more visually appealing. In the next section, we'll explore how to implement navigation drawers and bottom navigation for efficient app navigation.

Section 12.4: Navigation Drawer and Bottom Navigation

Navigation drawers and bottom navigation bars are essential UI components for building efficient and user-friendly Android apps. They provide intuitive ways for users to navigate between different sections of your app. In this section, we'll explore how to implement these two navigation patterns.

Navigation Drawer (DrawerLayout)

The navigation drawer, also known as a side menu or slide-out menu, is a panel that slides in from the side of the screen to reveal app navigation options. It's commonly used to display the app's main navigation menu.

Implementation Steps:

1. **Add Dependencies**: To use the Navigation Drawer, make sure to include the necessary AndroidX library in your `build.gradle` file:

   ```
   implementation 'androidx.drawerlayout:drawerlayout:1.1.1'
   ```

2. **Layout**: Create your layout XML file for the main activity, and include a `DrawerLayout` as the root view. Inside the `DrawerLayout`, you should have your main content view (e.g., a `FrameLayout`) and a navigation view (e.g., a `NavigationView`) for the drawer content.

   ```xml
   <androidx.drawerlayout.widget.DrawerLayout
       xmlns:android="http://schemas.android.com/apk/res/android"
       android:id="@+id/drawer_layout"
       android:layout_width="match_parent"
       android:layout_height="match_parent">

       <!-- Main content -->
       <FrameLayout
           android:id="@+id/main_content"
           android:layout_width="match_parent"
           android:layout_height="match_parent">
           <!-- Your app's content goes here -->
       </FrameLayout>

       <!-- Navigation drawer -->
       <com.google.android.material.navigation.NavigationView
           android:id="@+id/nav_view"
           android:layout_width="wrap_content"
           android:layout_height="match_parent"
           android:layout_gravity="start"
           app:menu="@menu/navigation_menu" />
   </androidx.drawerlayout.widget.DrawerLayout>
   ```

3. **Menu Items**: Create a menu resource file (e.g., `navigation_menu.xml`) to define the items in your navigation drawer.

```xml
<menu xmlns:android="http://schemas.android.com/apk/res/android">
    <item
        android:id="@+id/nav_home"
        android:title="Home" />
    <item
        android:id="@+id/nav_profile"
        android:title="Profile" />
    <!-- Add more items as needed -->
</menu>
```

4. **Toggle Button**: To open and close the navigation drawer, add a toggle button or icon in your app's toolbar or action bar. Use the `DrawerLayout` to toggle the drawer's visibility.

```kotlin
val drawerLayout = findViewById<DrawerLayout>(R.id.drawer_layout)
val toggle = ActionBarDrawerToggle(
    this,
    drawerLayout,
    R.string.navigation_drawer_open,
    R.string.navigation_drawer_close
)
drawerLayout.addDrawerListener(toggle)
toggle.syncState()
```

5. **Handling Item Selection**: Implement item selection logic for your navigation items. You can do this in your activity or fragment based on your app's structure.

```kotlin
val navView = findViewById<NavigationView>(R.id.nav_view)
navView.setNavigationItemSelectedListener { menuItem ->
    when (menuItem.itemId) {
        R.id.nav_home -> {
            // Handle Home click
            // Load the corresponding fragment or activity
            true
        }
        R.id.nav_profile -> {
            // Handle Profile click
            // Load the profile screen
            true
        }
        // Handle other menu items
        else -> false
    }
}
```

The bottom navigation bar is a common UI component that provides navigation options at the bottom of the screen. It's suitable for apps with a small number of primary destinations.

Implementation Steps:

1. **Layout**: Include a BottomNavigationView in your activity's layout XML file.

```
<com.google.android.material.bottomnavigation.BottomNavigationView
    android:id="@+id/bottom_nav_view"
    android:layout_width="match_parent"
    android:layout_height="wrap_content"
    android:layout_gravity="bottom"
    app:menu="@menu/bottom_navigation_menu" />
```

2. **Menu Items**: Create a menu resource file (e.g., bottom_navigation_menu.xml) to define the items in your bottom navigation bar.

```
<menu xmlns:android="http://schemas.android.com/apk/res/android">
    <item
        android:id="@+id/nav_home"
        android:title="Home"
        android:icon="@drawable/ic_home" />
    <item
        android:id="@+id/nav_explore"
        android:title="Explore"
        android:icon="@drawable/ic_explore" />
    <!-- Add more items as needed -->
</menu>
```

3. **Handling Item Selection**: Implement item selection logic for your bottom navigation items. Typically, this involves loading fragments or switching between different sections of your app.

```kotlin
val bottomNavView = findViewById(R.id.bottom_nav_view)
bottomNavView
```

Section 12.5: Creating Multi-screen Apps

Creating multi-screen apps is a fundamental aspect of Android app development. It allows you to build complex applications with various user interfaces and functionalities, enabling users to navigate seamlessly between different screens. In this section, we'll explore the key concepts and steps for creating multi-screen apps in Android.

Understanding Activities

In Android, each screen or UI component within your app is represented by an Activity. An Activity is a fundamental building block that provides a user interface and interacts with the user. Your app can consist of multiple activities, and each activity serves a specific purpose or displays a distinct UI.

Here are the essential concepts related to activities:

- **Activity Lifecycle**: Activities have a well-defined lifecycle, including methods like `onCreate()`, `onStart()`, `onResume()`, `onPause()`, `onStop()`, and `onDestroy()`. Understanding this lifecycle is crucial for managing the behavior of your app as the user navigates between screens.

- **Intent**: To move from one activity to another, you typically use an `Intent`. Intents can be explicit (targeting a specific activity) or implicit (indicating a type of action, and Android selects the appropriate activity).

Creating New Activities

To create a new activity in your Android project, follow these steps:

1. **Create a New Java or Kotlin Class**: In your Android Studio project, create a new Java or Kotlin class for your activity. Make sure it extends the `Activity` class.

2. **Define the Layout**: Create an XML layout file that defines the user interface for your activity. You can design it using the Layout Editor in Android Studio or write the XML manually.

3. **Configure the Manifest**: In the AndroidManifest.xml file, declare the new activity by adding an `<activity>` element inside the `<application>` element. Specify the activity's name and the associated layout.

```
<activity
    android:name=".YourActivityName"
    android:label="Activity Label">
    <intent-filter>
        <action android:name="android.intent.action.MAIN" />
        <category android:name="android.intent.category.LAUNCHER" />
    </intent-filter>
</activity>
```

4. **Start the New Activity**: To start the new activity, you can use an explicit intent. For example, if you're launching `YourActivityName`, use the following code in the source activity:

```
Intent intent = new Intent(this, YourActivityName.class);
startActivity(intent);
```

Passing Data Between Activities

In many cases, you'll need to pass data from one activity to another. You can achieve this using extras within your intent. Here's how you can send data:

```java
Intent intent = new Intent(this, AnotherActivity.class);
intent.putExtra("key", "value");
startActivity(intent);
```

And in the receiving activity, you can retrieve the data:

```java
Intent intent = getIntent();
String data = intent.getStringExtra("key");
```

Handling Back Navigation

By default, Android handles the back navigation for you, allowing users to return to the previous screen by pressing the back button. However, you can customize this behavior by overriding the `onBackPressed()` method within your activity.

Fragment-based UIs

While activities are used for navigation and managing the app's overall structure, you can use fragments to create reusable UI components within your activities. Fragments allow you to build flexible and modular user interfaces.

Navigation Components

Android's Navigation Architecture Component provides a more structured and declarative way to navigate between screens, manage the back stack, and handle deep linking. It simplifies the implementation of navigation in your app and encourages a more consistent user experience.

Testing and Debugging Multi-screen Apps

Testing multi-screen apps involves ensuring that activities transition correctly, data is passed accurately, and the app behaves as expected when the user navigates between screens. Android Studio provides various tools and emulators for testing and debugging your app's navigation and overall functionality.

In summary, creating multi-screen apps in Android involves designing activities, defining their layouts, handling navigation between them, passing data, and ensuring a smooth user experience. Understanding the activity lifecycle, intents, and navigation components is crucial for building robust and user-friendly Android applications.

Chapter 13: Working with Sensors and Hardware

In Chapter 13, we'll delve into the fascinating world of working with sensors and hardware in Android app development. Android devices come equipped with a variety of sensors and hardware components that can enrich your app's functionality and user experience. This chapter will explore how to access and utilize these sensors and hardware features effectively.

Section 13.1: Accessing Device Sensors

Device sensors play a vital role in enabling your Android app to interact with the physical world. Sensors can provide information about device orientation, motion, environmental conditions, and more. Here, we'll focus on how to access and use device sensors in your Android application.

Understanding Sensors in Android

Android devices come with a wide range of sensors, including:

- **Accelerometer**: Measures acceleration along three axes and is commonly used for detecting device orientation and motion.

- **Gyroscope**: Provides information about the device's angular velocity and is used in applications that require precise motion tracking.

- **Magnetometer (Compass)**: Measures the Earth's magnetic field, allowing your app to determine the device's orientation relative to the Earth's magnetic north.

- **Proximity Sensor**: Detects the presence of nearby objects and is often used to control the device's screen behavior during calls.

- **Light Sensor**: Measures ambient light levels and is used for tasks like adjusting screen brightness.

- **Barometer**: Measures atmospheric pressure and can be used to estimate altitude and weather conditions.

- **GPS (Global Positioning System)**: Provides accurate location information using satellite signals.

Using the SensorManager

To access device sensors, you'll primarily work with the `SensorManager` class. Here's how you can get started:

1. **Obtain the SensorManager**: You can obtain the `SensorManager` instance using the following code:

```
SensorManager sensorManager = (SensorManager) getSystemService(Context.
SENSOR_SERVICE);
```

2. **List Available Sensors**: You can list the available sensors on the device:

```
List<Sensor> sensorList = sensorManager.getSensorList(Sensor.TYPE_ALL);
```

This code retrieves a list of all available sensors. You can filter this list to access specific sensors like the accelerometer, gyroscope, or others.

3. **Register Sensor Listeners**: To receive sensor data, you'll need to register sensor listeners. Here's an example of registering an accelerometer sensor listener:

```
Sensor accelerometerSensor = sensorManager.getDefaultSensor(Sensor.TYPE
_ACCELEROMETER);
if (accelerometerSensor != null) {
    sensorManager.registerListener(accelerometerListener, accelerometer
Sensor, SensorManager.SENSOR_DELAY_NORMAL);
}
```

In this code, accelerometerListener is the listener you implement to handle sensor data, and SENSOR_DELAY_NORMAL specifies the data update rate.

4. **Implement Sensor Listeners**: Implementing sensor listeners involves defining the logic to handle sensor data. For example, with an accelerometer listener, you can monitor changes in device orientation and motion.

Handling Sensor Data

Handling sensor data often involves implementing the SensorEventListener interface. Here's a simplified example of how you might handle accelerometer data:

```
private SensorEventListener accelerometerListener = new SensorEventListener()
{
    @Override
    public void onSensorChanged(SensorEvent event) {
        float x = event.values[0];
        float y = event.values[1];
        float z = event.values[2];

        // Do something with accelerometer data (e.g., update UI)
    }

    @Override
    public void onAccuracyChanged(Sensor sensor, int accuracy) {
        // Handle accuracy changes if needed
    }
};
```

In the `onSensorChanged` method, you can access the sensor's data and use it to update your app's UI or perform other tasks based on the sensor's values.

It's important to consider sensor accuracy and power consumption when working with sensors. Some sensors may consume more power than others, and sensor accuracy can vary. Choose the most appropriate sensor for your app's specific requirements, and be mindful of power-efficient sensor usage.

In this section, you've learned the fundamentals of accessing device sensors in Android. We explored the types of sensors available, how to obtain the `SensorManager`, register sensor listeners, and handle sensor data. Understanding and effectively utilizing sensors can greatly enhance your app's capabilities and user experience, opening up possibilities for innovative applications.

Section 13.2: Working with GPS and Compass

In this section, we'll explore how to work with the GPS (Global Positioning System) and compass sensors in Android. These sensors enable your application to determine the device's geographic location and orientation, allowing you to create location-aware and navigation-based apps.

GPS (Global Positioning System)

GPS is a crucial sensor for location-based services. It provides accurate geographic coordinates (latitude, longitude), altitude, and sometimes speed information. Android offers a straightforward way to access GPS data.

To get started with GPS in Android, follow these steps:

1. **Request Permissions**: In your AndroidManifest.xml file, declare the necessary permissions for location access. For example:

   ```
   <uses-permission android:name="android.permission.ACCESS_FINE_LOCATION"
   />
   ```

   Use `ACCESS_FINE_LOCATION` for precise location access or `ACCESS_COARSE_LOCATION` for less accurate location data.

2. **Check Location Settings**: Before requesting location updates, check if location services are enabled on the device. You can use the `LocationManager` to check and request location updates:

   ```
   LocationManager locationManager = (LocationManager) getSystemService(Co
   ntext.LOCATION_SERVICE);
   boolean isGpsEnabled = locationManager.isProviderEnabled(LocationManage
   r.GPS_PROVIDER);
   ```

3. **Request Location Updates**: To receive location updates, you can use the requestLocationUpdates method. Specify the provider (e.g., GPS_PROVIDER), minimum time interval, and minimum distance interval:

```
locationManager.requestLocationUpdates(
    LocationManager.GPS_PROVIDER,
    MIN_TIME_INTERVAL,
    MIN_DISTANCE_INTERVAL,
    locationListener
);
```

The locationListener is an instance of LocationListener where you handle location updates.

4. **Implement LocationListener**: Implement the LocationListener interface to handle location updates. You'll override methods like onLocationChanged to process new location data.

```
private LocationListener locationListener = new LocationListener() {
    @Override
    public void onLocationChanged(Location location) {
        double latitude = location.getLatitude();
        double longitude = location.getLongitude();

        // Use location data for your app's functionality
    }

    // Other methods like onProviderEnabled, onProviderDisabled, onStatusChanged
};
```

5. **Location Providers**: Android provides different location providers, including GPS, network-based, and passive providers. You can choose the most appropriate provider based on your app's requirements.

Compass Sensor

The compass sensor, also known as the magnetometer, provides information about the device's orientation relative to the Earth's magnetic north. It's often used in apps that involve navigation or augmented reality.

To work with the compass sensor in Android:

1. **Request Permissions**: Declare the necessary permissions in your AndroidManifest.xml file, if not already done.

2. **Check Compass Availability**: Check if the device has a compass sensor available:

```
SensorManager sensorManager = (SensorManager) getSystemService(Context.SENSOR_SERVICE);
```

```
Sensor compassSensor = sensorManager.getDefaultSensor(Sensor.TYPE_MAGNE
TIC_FIELD);
```

Ensure that the compass sensor is not null before proceeding.

3. **Implement SensorEventListener**: Similar to working with other sensors, implement the `SensorEventListener` interface to handle compass data:

```
private SensorEventListener compassListener = new SensorEventListener()
{
    @Override
    public void onSensorChanged(SensorEvent event) {
        float azimuth = event.values[0];
        float pitch = event.values[1];
        float roll = event.values[2];

        // Use compass data for your app's functionality
    }

    @Override
    public void onAccuracyChanged(Sensor sensor, int accuracy) {
        // Handle accuracy changes if needed
    }
};
```

4. **Register and Unregister Listeners**: Register the compass sensor listener when your app needs compass data and unregister it when you no longer need updates. Be aware of power consumption when continuously using sensors.

These steps provide you with the basics of working with the GPS and compass sensors in Android. With these sensors, you can create applications ranging from location-based services to augmented reality experiences, enhancing your app's functionality and user engagement.

Section 13.3: Integrating NFC and Bluetooth

In this section, we'll delve into integrating Near Field Communication (NFC) and Bluetooth technologies into your Android applications. These technologies enable your apps to interact with nearby devices and objects, opening up possibilities for seamless data exchange and connectivity.

NFC (Near Field Communication)

NFC is a short-range wireless communication technology that allows devices to communicate when they are within a few centimeters of each other. It's commonly used for tasks like contactless payments, sharing files, and reading NFC tags. Here's how to work with NFC in Android:

1. **Check NFC Availability**: First, check if the device supports NFC by using the NfcAdapter class:

```
NfcAdapter nfcAdapter = NfcAdapter.getDefaultAdapter(this);
if (nfcAdapter == null) {
    // NFC is not available on this device
    // Handle this scenario in your app
}
```

2. **Request NFC Permissions**: Declare NFC permissions in your AndroidManifest.xml file:

```
<uses-permission android:name="android.permission.NFC" />
```

3. **Handle NFC Intent**: To react to NFC events, your activity should override the onNewIntent method:

```
@Override
protected void onNewIntent(Intent intent) {
    super.onNewIntent(intent);
    // Handle NFC intent here
}
```

   You can extract data from the NFC intent and perform actions based on the received data.

4. **Create NFC Tags**: If your app needs to create NFC tags for sharing data, you can use the NdefMessage class to define the data to be written to the tag.

5. **Read and Write NFC Tags**: Use the NfcAdapter to read and write data to NFC tags. When a user brings their device near an NFC tag, your app can respond and read the data or write new data to the tag.

Bluetooth

Bluetooth is a wireless technology for connecting devices over short distances. It's widely used for tasks like connecting to wireless headphones, speakers, and IoT devices. Here's how to work with Bluetooth in Android:

1. **Check Bluetooth Availability**: Ensure that Bluetooth is available on the device and enabled:

```
BluetoothAdapter bluetoothAdapter = BluetoothAdapter.getDefaultAdapter(
);
if (bluetoothAdapter == null) {
    // Bluetooth is not available on this device
    // Handle this scenario in your app
} else {
    if (!bluetoothAdapter.isEnabled()) {
        // Bluetooth is available but not enabled
```

```
        // Prompt the user to enable Bluetooth
    }
}
```

2. **Request Bluetooth Permissions**: Declare Bluetooth permissions in your
   AndroidManifest.xml file:

```
<uses-permission android:name="android.permission.BLUETOOTH" />
<uses-permission android:name="android.permission.BLUETOOTH_ADMIN" />
```

   Additionally, if your app targets Android 12 or later, you'll need the `BLUETOOTH_SCAN`
   permission for scanning nearby devices.

3. **Discover Nearby Bluetooth Devices**: Use the `BluetoothAdapter` to discover
   nearby Bluetooth devices, pair with them, and establish connections.

4. **Implement Bluetooth Profiles**: Depending on your use case, you might need to
   implement specific Bluetooth profiles like A2DP for audio streaming or GATT for
   Bluetooth Low Energy (BLE) communication.

5. **Handle Bluetooth Connections**: Manage Bluetooth connections, including
   connecting, disconnecting, and transferring data between devices.

Integrating NFC and Bluetooth capabilities into your Android app can greatly enhance its
functionality and enable it to interact with other devices and objects in the physical world.
Whether you're building a contactless payment app, a file-sharing utility, or a device
control application, understanding these technologies is valuable for creating seamless
user experiences.

Section 13.4: Accessing Device Hardware

In this section, we'll explore how to access various hardware components of an Android
device in your application. Android provides APIs to interact with hardware features like
the camera, sensors, GPS, and more, enabling you to create versatile and feature-rich
applications.

Accessing the Camera

Accessing the device's camera is a common requirement for many Android apps, especially
those that involve photography, video recording, or augmented reality. To access the
camera, follow these steps:

1. **Check Camera Availability**: First, you should check if the device has a camera:

```
if (getPackageManager().hasSystemFeature(PackageManager.FEATURE_CAMERA)
) {
    // The device has a camera
}
```

2. **Request Camera Permissions**: Declare camera permissions in your AndroidManifest.xml file:

```
<uses-permission android:name="android.permission.CAMERA" />
```

3. **Open the Camera**: You can use the Camera or Camera2 API to open and interact with the device's camera. Ensure that you handle camera resource management and release it properly when not in use.

4. **Capture Photos or Record Video**: Depending on your app's requirements, you can capture photos or record video using the camera API.

5. **Implement Camera Preview**: If you want to display a live camera preview in your app, create a SurfaceView or a TextureView to display what the camera sees.

Working with Sensors

Android devices are equipped with various sensors like accelerometers, gyroscopes, proximity sensors, and ambient light sensors. Here's how to work with sensors in your app:

1. **Check Sensor Availability**: Check if a specific sensor is available on the device:

```
SensorManager sensorManager = (SensorManager) getSystemService(Context.
SENSOR_SERVICE);
Sensor accelerometerSensor = sensorManager.getDefaultSensor(Sensor.TYPE
_ACCELEROMETER);
if (accelerometerSensor != null) {
    // The accelerometer sensor is available
}
```

2. **Register Sensor Listeners**: Register sensor listeners to receive data from sensors. Implement the SensorEventListener interface to handle sensor events.

```
SensorEventListener sensorEventListener = new SensorEventListener() {
    @Override
    public void onSensorChanged(SensorEvent event) {
        // Handle sensor data here
    }

    @Override
    public void onAccuracyChanged(Sensor sensor, int accuracy) {
        // Handle accuracy changes here
    }
};
sensorManager.registerListener(sensorEventListener, accelerometerSensor
, SensorManager.SENSOR_DELAY_NORMAL);
```

3. **Unregister Sensor Listeners**: Don't forget to unregister sensor listeners when they are no longer needed to conserve battery life:

```
sensorManager.unregisterListener(sensorEventListener);
```

Accessing location information is crucial for location-based applications, navigation apps, and services. Android provides Location APIs to retrieve the device's current location. Here's how to work with location services:

1. **Check Location Services Availability**: Verify that location services are enabled on the device and request permissions in your AndroidManifest.xml file:

   ```
   <uses-permission android:name="android.permission.ACCESS_FINE_LOCATION"
   />
   ```

2. **Request Location Updates**: Use the LocationManager or the newer FusedLocationProviderClient to request location updates. Define a location listener to handle location data as it becomes available.

3. **Handle Location Updates**: Implement the location listener's onLocationChanged method to process location updates.

4. **Geocoding and Reverse Geocoding**: You can use the Geocoding API to convert between geographic coordinates (latitude and longitude) and human-readable addresses. Reverse geocoding allows you to obtain an address from coordinates, while geocoding does the opposite.

By understanding and utilizing these hardware access techniques, you can create Android apps that interact with the device's camera, sensors, GPS, and other hardware components effectively. These capabilities open up a wide range of possibilities for innovative and feature-rich applications.

Section 13.5: Building IoT and Wearable Apps

In this section, we'll delve into the world of IoT (Internet of Things) and wearable app development on the Android platform. These types of apps interact with external devices, such as smart home appliances, fitness trackers, smartwatches, and more. Building IoT and wearable apps allows you to create applications that bridge the gap between the digital and physical worlds.

IoT App Development

IoT refers to the network of interconnected physical devices that can communicate and exchange data. Android provides several tools and libraries to develop IoT applications that control and monitor IoT devices. Here are key steps in IoT app development:

1. **Device Communication Protocols**: IoT devices often use communication protocols like MQTT, CoAP, or HTTP to send and receive data. Implement the appropriate protocol in your app to communicate with the devices.

2. **IoT SDKs and Libraries**: Leverage IoT SDKs and libraries provided by device manufacturers or third-party providers to simplify device integration. These SDKs often contain APIs for device discovery, control, and data retrieval.

3. **Security**: Security is paramount in IoT app development. Implement strong authentication, encryption, and authorization mechanisms to protect data and device access.

4. **User Interface**: Design an intuitive user interface (UI) that allows users to interact with and control IoT devices. This might include real-time data visualization, control buttons, and notifications.

5. **Cloud Integration**: Many IoT apps use cloud platforms like AWS IoT, Google Cloud IoT, or Microsoft Azure IoT to manage devices and data. Integrate your app with these platforms for scalability and remote device management.

Wearable App Development

Wearable devices, such as smartwatches and fitness trackers, have gained popularity in recent years. Android provides the Wear OS platform for developing apps for wearable devices. Here's how to get started with wearable app development:

1. **Wearable App Project**: Create a new Android Studio project with Wear OS support to start building a wearable app.

2. **User Notifications**: Wearable apps often rely on notifications to keep users informed. Design interactive and glanceable notifications for the wearable device's small screen.

3. **Data Synchronization**: If your wearable app collects or displays data, ensure that it synchronizes seamlessly with the companion mobile app. Use the Wearable Data Layer API for data exchange.

4. **User Input**: Consider how users will interact with the wearable app. Depending on the device, this could involve touch gestures, voice commands, or physical buttons.

5. **Battery Optimization**: Optimize your app for battery efficiency. Wearable devices typically have limited battery life, so efficient coding practices are essential.

6. **Testing on Wearable Emulators**: Android Studio provides wearable emulators for testing your app's behavior on various Wear OS devices.

7. **Companion Mobile App**: Many wearable apps have a companion mobile app that handles configuration, data synchronization, and extended features. Ensure smooth communication between the wearable and mobile components.

8. **Deployment**: Publish your wearable app on the Google Play Store, ensuring that it's compatible with the intended wearable devices.

Developing IoT and wearable apps opens up exciting possibilities for innovation. Whether you're controlling smart home devices, tracking fitness goals, or creating unique wearable experiences, Android provides the tools and resources needed to bring these applications to life. Remember to consider the specific requirements and limitations of the IoT or wearable device you're targeting to create a seamless user experience.

Chapter 14: Background Processing and Services

Section 14.1: Understanding Background Processing

In the world of Android app development, background processing plays a crucial role in ensuring that your application runs smoothly and efficiently. Background processing refers to the execution of tasks or operations that don't require the immediate attention of the user and can be performed outside of the app's main user interface. This allows your app to remain responsive while handling tasks such as data synchronization, updates, and maintenance in the background.

Why Background Processing is Important

Background processing is essential for several reasons:

1. **User Experience**: Background processing ensures that the user interface remains responsive and doesn't freeze or lag while performing time-consuming tasks. This contributes to a better overall user experience.

2. **Data Synchronization**: Many apps need to synchronize data with remote servers or fetch updates in the background. This is crucial for apps like email clients, social media apps, and news readers.

3. **Notifications**: Background processing enables apps to deliver timely notifications, such as messages, reminders, and updates, even when the app is not actively in use.

4. **Battery Optimization**: Properly designed background tasks can help conserve battery life by minimizing CPU and network usage when the device is not actively being used.

5. **Offline Access**: Background processing can also help in pre-fetching data for offline access, ensuring that users can continue to use certain features even without an internet connection.

Types of Background Processing

In Android, there are several mechanisms for implementing background processing:

1. **Background Threads**: You can create and manage background threads to perform tasks concurrently with the main thread. However, you need to be cautious about managing thread lifecycles and preventing issues like memory leaks.

2. **AsyncTask**: AsyncTask is a convenient way to perform background operations and publish results on the UI thread. It simplifies thread management but may not be suitable for long-running tasks.

3. **Services**: Android Services are components that can run in the background, independently of the app's user interface. They are often used for tasks that need to run continuously or periodically, such as music playback or location tracking.

4. **WorkManager**: WorkManager is a modern Android library that simplifies the scheduling of background tasks. It provides an easy-to-use API for defining and running deferrable and guaranteed background work.

5. **JobScheduler**: JobScheduler is another Android framework feature that allows you to schedule tasks to run when specific conditions are met, such as when the device is charging or connected to Wi-Fi.

Best Practices for Background Processing

To ensure that your app's background processing is efficient and doesn't negatively impact the user experience, consider the following best practices:

- **Use the Right Mechanism**: Choose the background processing mechanism that best suits your task's requirements. For example, use WorkManager for tasks that can be deferred and scheduled.

- **Minimize Wake Locks**: Avoid holding wake locks for extended periods, as this can lead to increased battery usage. Release wake locks as soon as they are no longer needed.

- **Network Access**: Be mindful of network usage in the background. Perform network operations judiciously, and consider batching them to minimize data transfer.

- **Foreground Service**: If your app needs to perform a task that's critical to the user experience, consider using a Foreground Service, which provides a persistent notification to the user and is less likely to be killed by the system.

- **Testing**: Test your app's background processing thoroughly, including scenarios like interruptions, low memory conditions, and different Android versions.

- **Error Handling**: Implement robust error handling and retry mechanisms for background tasks to handle unexpected situations gracefully.

- **Battery Optimization**: Respect Android's battery optimization features and guidelines to ensure your app is power-efficient.

Understanding and effectively implementing background processing is crucial for building responsive and user-friendly Android applications. It enables your app to perform tasks efficiently while maintaining a smooth user experience, ultimately leading to higher user satisfaction and retention.

Section 14.2: Creating Background Services

In Android, background services are essential components for performing tasks that require continuous or periodic execution, even when the app's user interface is not visible. Services are a fundamental part of Android's background processing capabilities, and they are designed to run independently and perform long-running operations without blocking the main UI thread.

Creating a Background Service

To create a background service in Android, you need to follow these steps:

1. **Create a Service Class**: Start by creating a Java or Kotlin class that extends the Service class or its subclasses (IntentService or JobService). This class will define the logic of your background service.

2. **Override onCreate Method**: In your service class, override the onCreate method. This method is called when the service is initially created. You can perform any one-time initialization tasks here.

3. **Override onStartCommand Method**: This method is called every time a client (usually an activity or another component) starts the service using startService(). You should implement the background task logic here. Be sure to return an appropriate value, such as START_STICKY, which tells the system to restart the service if it's killed.

4. **Implement Background Task**: Inside the onStartCommand method, you can implement the specific background task your service needs to perform. This could be anything from downloading data from the internet to processing data in the background.

5. **Stop the Service**: Once your background task is complete, you can stop the service by calling stopSelf() from within the service class. This allows the service to gracefully shut down.

6. **Manifest Declaration**: Don't forget to declare your service in the AndroidManifest.xml file. This tells Android about your service and allows other components to start it.

Here's a simplified example of a background service that periodically logs a message:

```
import android.app.Service;
import android.content.Intent;
import android.os.Handler;
import android.os.IBinder;
import android.util.Log;
```

```java
public class MyBackgroundService extends Service {

    private static final String TAG = "MyBackgroundService";
    private Handler handler;
    private Runnable periodicTask;

    @Override
    public void onCreate() {
        super.onCreate();
        handler = new Handler();
        periodicTask = new Runnable() {
            @Override
            public void run() {
                Log.d(TAG, "Background Service is running");
                // Perform your background task here
                handler.postDelayed(this, 5000); // Run every 5 seconds
            }
        };
    }

    @Override
    public int onStartCommand(Intent intent, int flags, int startId) {
        handler.post(periodicTask); // Start the periodic task
        return START_STICKY; // Service will be restarted if killed by the system
    }

    @Override
    public void onDestroy() {
        super.onDestroy();
        handler.removeCallbacks(periodicTask); // Stop the periodic task
    }

    @Override
    public IBinder onBind(Intent intent) {
        // Not used in this example
        return null;
    }
}
```

Starting and Stopping a Service

To start a background service, you can use the `startService()` method, passing an intent that identifies the service class. For example:

```java
Intent serviceIntent = new Intent(this, MyBackgroundService.class);
startService(serviceIntent);
```

To stop a service, you can use the `stopService()` method:

```java
Intent serviceIntent = new Intent(this, MyBackgroundService.class);
stopService(serviceIntent);
```

Services are a powerful tool for background processing in Android, but they come with responsibilities. It's crucial to manage the lifecycle of your service properly, ensure it doesn't drain the device's resources unnecessarily, and handle errors gracefully. When used correctly, services can enhance the functionality and user experience of your Android app by enabling it to perform tasks efficiently in the background.

Section 14.3: Scheduling Background Tasks

In Android, scheduling background tasks is a common requirement for many apps. Whether you need to update data, send notifications, or perform other periodic tasks, Android provides several mechanisms for scheduling background tasks. In this section, we will explore some of the approaches to scheduling tasks in the background.

1. AlarmManager

The AlarmManager is a powerful system service that allows you to schedule tasks to be executed at specified times or intervals, even if your app is not running. It's particularly useful for scenarios like triggering notifications or syncing data periodically.

Here's an example of how to use AlarmManager to schedule a task:

```java
// Get the AlarmManager service
AlarmManager alarmManager = (AlarmManager) getSystemService(Context.ALARM_SERVICE);

// Create an intent to specify the task to be performed
Intent intent = new Intent(this, MyAlarmReceiver.class);

// Create a PendingIntent to wrap the intent
PendingIntent pendingIntent = PendingIntent.getBroadcast(this, 0, intent, 0);

// Set the time when the task should run (e.g., every hour)
long intervalMillis = AlarmManager.INTERVAL_HOUR;
long triggerAtMillis = System.currentTimeMillis() + intervalMillis;

// Schedule the task
alarmManager.setInexactRepeating(AlarmManager.RTC_WAKEUP, triggerAtMillis, intervalMillis, pendingIntent);
```

In this example, we create an Intent that specifies the task to be performed and wrap it in a PendingIntent. We then use setInexactRepeating() to schedule the task to run at regular intervals.

2. WorkManager

WorkManager is a modern and recommended way to schedule background tasks, especially for tasks that require guaranteed execution, even if the app is in the background or the device restarts. It offers features like task retry, network constraints, and battery optimizations.

Here's a basic example of how to use WorkManager to schedule a simple task:

```
// Define the work request
OneTimeWorkRequest workRequest = new OneTimeWorkRequest.Builder(MyWorkerClass
.class).build();

// Enqueue the work request
WorkManager.getInstance(this).enqueue(workRequest);
```

In this code, we create a WorkRequest and enqueue it using WorkManager. You also need to create a Worker class (MyWorkerClass in this case) that defines the task to be executed.

3. JobScheduler

JobScheduler is another option for scheduling background tasks, and it provides fine-grained control over task scheduling based on conditions like network connectivity and charging status. It's suitable for tasks that can be deferred and batched for more efficient execution.

Here's an example of how to use JobScheduler to schedule a task:

```
// Get the JobScheduler service
JobScheduler jobScheduler = (JobScheduler) getSystemService(Context.JOB_SCHED
ULER_SERVICE);

// Create a JobInfo.Builder to define the job
JobInfo.Builder builder = new JobInfo.Builder(JOB_ID, new ComponentName(this,
MyJobService.class));

// Set scheduling conditions (e.g., network connectivity)
builder.setRequiredNetworkType(JobInfo.NETWORK_TYPE_ANY);

// Set the periodic interval (e.g., every 30 minutes)
builder.setPeriodic(30 * 60 * 1000);

// Schedule the job
jobScheduler.schedule(builder.build());
```

In this example, we use JobScheduler to define a job with specific conditions and a periodic interval. You also need to create a JobService (MyJobService in this case) that defines the task to be executed.

For simple tasks that need to be run on the main thread periodically, you can use a `Handler` and `Runnable`. While this approach is not suitable for long-running or network-related tasks, it's handy for updating UI elements or running lightweight operations.

Here's an example:

```
Handler handler = new Handler();
Runnable runnable = new Runnable() {
    @Override
    public void run() {
        // Your periodic task
        handler.postDelayed(this, 10000); // Run every 10 seconds
    }
};

handler.post(runnable);
```

In this code, we use a `Handler` to run a `Runnable` periodically on the main thread.

These are some of the methods you can use to schedule background tasks in Android. The choice of which method to use depends on your app's specific requirements and the nature of the tasks you need to perform. It's essential to select the right approach to ensure efficient and reliable background task execution.

Section 14.4: Sync Adapters and Data Syncing

Syncing data between your Android app and a remote server is a common requirement. It ensures that your app always has access to the latest data and can work offline. Android provides a powerful mechanism called **Sync Adapters** to handle data synchronization efficiently.

1. Understanding Sync Adapters

A Sync Adapter is a component that allows your app to sync data between the device and a server. It runs in the background, and Android manages when and how often it syncs data. Sync Adapters are ideal for handling periodic or on-demand data synchronization.

2. Creating a Sync Adapter

To create a Sync Adapter, you need to perform the following steps:

Step 1: Define the Sync Adapter

You define your Sync Adapter by extending the `AbstractThreadedSyncAdapter` class and implementing the necessary methods:

```java
public class MySyncAdapter extends AbstractThreadedSyncAdapter {
    // Constructor
    public MySyncAdapter(Context context, boolean autoInitialize) {
        super(context, autoInitialize);
    }

    @Override
    public void onPerformSync(Account account, Bundle extras, String authorit
y, ContentProviderClient provider, SyncResult syncResult) {
        // Perform data synchronization here
    }
}
```

Step 2: Declare the Sync Adapter in AndroidManifest.xml

You must declare your Sync Adapter in the AndroidManifest.xml file:

```xml
<service
    android:name=".sync.MySyncAdapter"
    android:exported="true"
    android:process=":sync">
    <intent-filter>
        <action android:name="android.content.SyncAdapter" />
    </intent-filter>
    <meta-data
        android:name="android.content.SyncAdapter"
        android:resource="@xml/sync_adapter" />
</service>
```

Step 3: Define Sync Adapter Metadata

Create an XML resource file (e.g., `res/xml/sync_adapter.xml`) to define metadata for your Sync Adapter:

```xml
<?xml version="1.0" encoding="utf-8"?>
<sync-adapter xmlns:android="http://schemas.android.com/apk/res/android"
    android:contentAuthority="com.example.provider"
    android:accountType="com.example.account"
    android:userVisible="true"
    android:supportsUploading="false"
    android:allowParallelSyncs="false"
    android:isAlwaysSyncable="true"
    android:syncAdapterSettingsActivity="com.example.SyncSettingsActivity" />
```

Step 4: Request Sync

To trigger a sync operation, use the following code:

```java
// Request a sync for a specific account and authority
Account account = new Account("accountName", "accountType");
ContentResolver.requestSync(account, authority, new Bundle());
```

3. Handling Data Syncing

Inside the `onPerformSync` method of your Sync Adapter, you can implement the logic to synchronize data with your server. This can include downloading new data, uploading changes, or resolving conflicts.

4. Sync Adapter Configuration

You can configure various aspects of your Sync Adapter, such as the synchronization frequency and whether it should work on metered networks, in the metadata defined in the `sync_adapter.xml` file.

5. Authenticating with Accounts

Sync Adapters often work with user accounts. Ensure that you have implemented proper authentication and account management in your app.

6. Handling Errors and Conflicts

Sync Adapters should handle errors gracefully and be prepared to handle conflicts that may arise during data synchronization.

7. Efficient Data Transfer

Efficiency is crucial when syncing data. Use compression, batching, and intelligent syncing strategies to minimize data transfer and conserve battery life.

8. Battery Optimization

Scheduling syncs at the right times and optimizing data transfer can significantly reduce the impact on the device's battery.

Sync Adapters are a robust solution for data synchronization, allowing your Android app to stay up-to-date with server data efficiently. When implemented correctly, they ensure a seamless user experience, even in offline scenarios.

Section 14.5: Optimizing Battery Usage

Optimizing battery usage is a critical aspect of Android app development. Mobile devices rely on battery power, and inefficient apps can drain a user's battery quickly, leading to a poor user experience and negative reviews. This section explores various techniques and best practices for optimizing battery usage in your Android apps.

1. Minimize Background Processing

One of the primary culprits of battery drain is excessive background processing. To minimize this:

- **Use AlarmManager Sparingly:** AlarmManager can schedule periodic tasks, but overuse can lead to frequent wake-ups and battery drain. Consider alternatives like JobScheduler or WorkManager, which batch tasks for more efficient execution.

- **Background Services:** Avoid running long-lived background services unnecessarily. Use foreground services when needed and stop them when the task is complete.

2. Efficient Networking

Networking operations can significantly impact battery life. To optimize:

- **Batch Network Requests:** Combine multiple network requests into a single batch to reduce the number of radio wake-ups.

- **Use Doze and App Standby Modes:** Android's Doze and App Standby modes restrict background network activity, helping to conserve battery.

3. Location Services

Location updates can be a significant battery drain. Optimize location-related features:

- **Request Updates Strategically:** Request location updates at longer intervals when high precision isn't necessary.

- **Geofencing:** Use geofencing with care, as it can lead to frequent location checks. Combine geofencing with other sensors or limit checks to conserve battery.

4. Wake Locks

Avoid using wake locks unnecessarily, as they prevent the device from entering low-power states. Release wake locks as soon as they're no longer needed.

5. Optimize UI Rendering

Efficient UI rendering is crucial for battery life. Use hardware acceleration and minimize view redraws. Implement custom views with onDraw() when complex rendering is required.

6. Efficient Data Structures

Choose data structures and algorithms that minimize CPU and memory usage. Be mindful of excessive object creation and garbage collection.

7. Background Tasks

Use background tasks, such as AsyncTask or coroutines, for time-consuming operations that don't require immediate user interaction. These tasks run on worker threads, reducing the impact on the UI thread.

8. Battery Profiling

Use Android Profiler to profile your app's battery usage. Identify areas where excessive CPU, network, or wake locks are causing battery drain.

9. Optimize for Doze Mode

Android's Doze mode restricts background activity to save battery. Ensure your app works effectively in this mode by using the Network and Wake locks efficiently.

10. Battery Historian

Use the Battery Historian tool to analyze battery usage data. It provides insights into which app components are consuming power and helps pinpoint optimization opportunities.

11. Background Limits

Adhere to Android's background execution limits introduced in newer versions. Background apps have restricted access to system resources, which can impact their functionality but improves battery life.

12. User Settings

Allow users to customize app settings related to battery optimization, such as sync frequency, notifications, and background data usage.

13. Regular Testing

Regularly test your app on different devices and Android versions to ensure it behaves efficiently and doesn't drain battery excessively.

Battery optimization is an ongoing process in Android development. By implementing these best practices and staying up-to-date with Android's evolving power management features, you can create apps that are both efficient and user-friendly, contributing to a positive user experience.

Chapter 15: App Monetization and Distribution

Section 15.1: Monetization Strategies

App monetization is a crucial aspect of the app development process. It involves generating revenue from your mobile application. There are several strategies to monetize your app, and choosing the right one depends on your target audience, app niche, and business goals. In this section, we'll explore various monetization strategies for your Android app.

1. Freemium Model

The freemium model offers a basic version of your app for free, with the option to purchase premium features or content through in-app purchases. This model allows you to acquire a large user base and generate revenue from a subset of users who choose to upgrade. Implementing this strategy requires careful planning of what features to offer for free and what to reserve for paid users.

2. In-App Advertising

In-app advertising involves displaying ads within your app. You can earn revenue through various ad formats, such as banner ads, interstitial ads, rewarded videos, and native ads. Popular ad networks like Google AdMob and Facebook Audience Network make it easy to integrate ads into your app. However, striking a balance between ads and user experience is crucial to prevent user frustration.

3. In-App Purchases (IAP)

In-app purchases allow users to buy virtual goods, premium content, or subscriptions within your app. This strategy is commonly used in games and content-based apps. Effective pricing, clear value propositions, and providing regular updates with new content are essential to keep users engaged and willing to make purchases.

4. Subscription Model

The subscription model involves offering access to your app's premium features or content on a recurring basis. This approach is suitable for apps that provide ongoing value, such as streaming services, news apps, or productivity tools. Implementing subscriptions requires managing user billing and providing consistent value to retain subscribers.

5. Selling Digital Products

If your app provides a platform for users to sell their digital products or services, you can take a commission from each transaction. E-commerce apps and marketplaces often follow this monetization strategy. Building trust and security features are crucial for the success of this model.

6. Affiliate Marketing

Affiliate marketing involves promoting third-party products or services within your app and earning a commission for each sale or action generated through your referral. This strategy works well for apps with a relevant audience and can be integrated into content-driven apps or review platforms.

7. Sponsorship and Partnerships

Collaborating with sponsors or partners can be a lucrative monetization strategy. You can feature sponsored content, conduct co-marketing campaigns, or offer exclusive deals to your users. Building strong relationships with partners is key to the success of this approach.

8. Donations and Crowdfunding

For apps with a loyal user base, accepting donations or crowdfunding can be a sustainable way to generate revenue. Platforms like Patreon and Kickstarter can help you set up donation-based monetization. Offering unique perks or rewards to donors can incentivize contributions.

9. Pay-Per-Download (Paid App)

Requiring users to pay a one-time fee to download your app is a straightforward monetization method. However, it can limit your user base compared to free apps. To succeed with this model, your app must offer exceptional value to justify the upfront cost.

10. Combination of Strategies

In practice, many successful apps use a combination of these monetization strategies to diversify their revenue streams. Choosing the right combination depends on your app's unique value proposition and target audience.

When selecting a monetization strategy, it's essential to consider user experience, transparency, and providing value to your users. Additionally, staying updated with industry trends and continuously optimizing your monetization strategy can lead to long-term success.

Remember that successful monetization often requires experimentation and adaptation based on user feedback and market dynamics.

Section 15.2: In-App Advertising

In-app advertising is a widely used monetization strategy for mobile apps. It involves displaying advertisements within your app's interface. There are various ad formats and ad networks available for Android developers to choose from. In this section, we'll explore in-app advertising, its benefits, and how to integrate ads into your Android app.

1. **Revenue Generation**: In-app advertising provides a steady stream of income for app developers. You earn money when users view or interact with ads.

2. **Free App Model**: You can offer your app for free to a broader audience, increasing its user base and potential for ad revenue.

3. **User Engagement**: Well-placed and relevant ads can enhance user engagement. For example, a gaming app can display rewarded video ads that offer in-game rewards, encouraging users to interact with ads.

4. **Flexible Implementation**: In-app advertising allows for flexibility in implementation. You can choose the ad formats and placements that best suit your app's design and user experience.

1. **Banner Ads**: Banner ads are rectangular ads displayed at the top or bottom of the screen. They are less intrusive but may have lower click-through rates (CTR).

2. **Interstitial Ads**: Interstitial ads are full-screen ads that appear at natural breaks in your app's content, such as between levels in a game.

3. **Rewarded Video Ads**: These ads offer users a reward, such as in-game currency or an extra life, in exchange for watching a video ad. They are highly effective in engaging users.

4. **Native Ads**: Native ads are designed to match the app's visual and functional design, providing a seamless user experience. They blend in with the app's content.

5. **Playable Ads**: Common in gaming apps, playable ads allow users to interact with a mini-version of a game before downloading it.

To integrate in-app ads into your Android app, follow these general steps:

1. Choose an Ad Network

Select an ad network that suits your app's audience and objectives. Popular ad networks include Google AdMob, Facebook Audience Network, and Unity Ads.

2. Create an Ad Unit

Create an ad unit in your chosen ad network's dashboard. This unit represents the ad space in your app.

3. Add the SDK

Integrate the ad network's SDK into your Android project. You'll find detailed instructions in the network's documentation.

Decide where to display ads in your app. Common placements include banner ads at the top or bottom of screens, interstitial ads between content, or rewarded video ads after specific actions.

5. Load and Display Ads

Load ads from the ad unit and display them in your app. Most ad networks provide code snippets for loading and displaying ads.

Here's a simplified example of loading and displaying a banner ad using Google AdMob:

```
// Initialize AdMob
MobileAds.initialize(context, initializationStatus -> {});

// Create an ad view
AdView adView = new AdView(context);
adView.setAdSize(AdSize.BANNER);
adView.setAdUnitId("your_ad_unit_id");

// Add the ad view to your layout
ViewGroup layout = findViewById(R.id.adLayout);
layout.addView(adView);

// Load the ad
AdRequest adRequest = new AdRequest.Builder().build();
adView.loadAd(adRequest);
```

6. Handle Ad Events

Implement event handlers to handle ad events such as clicks, impressions, and reward callbacks (for rewarded video ads).

7. Test Your Implementation

Before publishing your app, thoroughly test your ad implementation to ensure that ads display correctly and do not interfere with the user experience.

In-app advertising can be a lucrative monetization strategy when implemented thoughtfully. Ensure that ads are relevant to your audience and do not disrupt the user experience, as a poor ad experience can lead to app abandonment. Regularly review ad performance and make adjustments as needed to optimize revenue and user satisfaction.

Section 15.3: Implementing In-App Purchases

In-app purchases (IAPs) are a common monetization strategy for Android apps that allow users to buy digital content or features within an app. This can include items like virtual goods, premium content, or ad removal. In this section, we'll explore how to implement in-app purchases in your Android app using Google Play Billing.

Benefits of In-App Purchases

Implementing in-app purchases offers several advantages:

1. **Diverse Monetization**: You can offer a range of products or services, giving users choices in how they want to support your app.

2. **Higher Revenue**: Users are more likely to spend money on a product they can try before buying. In-app purchases allow users to access premium content or features temporarily, increasing the likelihood of purchase.

3. **Continuous Revenue Stream**: You can generate a continuous stream of income as users make additional purchases or renew subscriptions.

4. **Free App Adoption**: You can offer your app for free and provide essential features, allowing users to upgrade through in-app purchases.

Implementing In-App Purchases

To implement in-app purchases in your Android app, follow these steps:

1. Set Up Google Play Console
- Go to the Google Play Console.
- Create a developer account if you don't have one.
- Create a new app listing or use an existing one.

2. Create Products
- In the Play Console, navigate to "Monetize" > "In-app products."
- Create the in-app products you want to sell. This could be items, subscriptions, or consumables.
- Define product details, pricing, and availability.

3. Integrate Google Play Billing Library
- Add the Google Play Billing Library to your Android project's dependencies.

```
implementation 'com.android.billingclient:billing:4.0.0'
```

4. Implement the Billing Flow
- Create a BillingClient instance and establish a connection to Google Play Billing.

```
// Create a BillingClient instance
BillingClient billingClient = BillingClient.newBuilder(context)
    .setListener(purchasesUpdatedListener)
    .build();

// Connect to Google Play Billing
```

```
billingClient.startConnection(connectionResult -> {
    if (connectionResult.getResponseCode() == BillingClient.BillingResp
onseCode.OK) {
        // BillingClient is ready
    }
});
```

5. Query for Available Products

- Use the BillingClient to query for available in-app products.

```
List<String> skuList = Arrays.asList("product_id_1", "product_id_2");
SkuDetailsParams.Builder params = SkuDetailsParams.newBuilder();
params.setSkusList(skuList).setType(BillingClient.SkuType.INAPP);

billingClient.querySkuDetailsAsync(params.build(), (billingResult, skuD
etailsList) -> {
    if (billingResult.getResponseCode() == BillingClient.BillingRespons
eCode.OK && skuDetailsList != null) {
        // Handle the list of available products
    }
});
```

6. Launch the Purchase Flow

- When a user wants to make a purchase, initiate the purchase flow.

```
BillingFlowParams.Builder builder = BillingFlowParams.newBuilder()
    .setSkuDetails(skuDetails); // Pass the SkuDetails for the product
int responseCode = billingClient.launchBillingFlow(activity, builder.bu
ild());
```

7. Handle Purchase Results

- Implement the PurchasesUpdatedListener to handle purchase results.

```
PurchasesUpdatedListener purchasesUpdatedListener = (billingResult, pur
chases) -> {
    if (billingResult.getResponseCode() == BillingClient.BillingRespons
eCode.OK && purchases != null) {
        // Handle the successful purchase
    }
};
```

8. Consumable and Subscription Products

- Implement logic to handle consumable products (e.g., virtual currency) and subscription renewals as per your app's requirements.

9. Testing

- Test your in-app purchase implementation using test accounts and the Google Play Console's testing tools.

- Once you've thoroughly tested your in-app purchases, you can publish your app to the Google Play Store.

Implementing in-app purchases requires careful planning and testing to ensure a smooth user experience. It's important to provide clear and transparent pricing information to users and to handle purchases and subscriptions securely. Regularly monitor and maintain your in-app purchase implementation to ensure it remains functional and compliant with Google Play policies.

Section 15.4: Preparing Your App for the Play Store

Once you've developed and thoroughly tested your Android app, the next step is to prepare it for distribution on the Google Play Store. This section will guide you through the necessary steps to get your app ready for the Play Store, ensuring that it meets all requirements and provides a smooth user experience.

1. App Testing and Quality Assurance

Before publishing your app, it's crucial to perform comprehensive testing and quality assurance to identify and fix any bugs, crashes, or usability issues. Here are some essential testing steps:

- **Functional Testing**: Ensure that all app features work as intended.
- **Compatibility Testing**: Test your app on various Android devices and screen sizes.
- **User Interface Testing**: Check for consistent and intuitive UI/UX design.
- **Performance Testing**: Optimize your app for smooth performance and fast load times.
- **Security Testing**: Verify that your app is secure and handles user data appropriately.

2. App Optimization

Optimizing your app for the Play Store can improve its visibility and discoverability. Here are some optimization tips:

- **App Title and Description**: Use clear, concise, and informative titles and descriptions.
- **Keywords**: Include relevant keywords in your app's description and metadata.
- **Screenshots and Videos**: Add high-quality screenshots and videos that showcase your app's features.
- **App Icon**: Design an attractive and recognizable app icon.
- **User Ratings and Reviews**: Encourage users to rate and review your app positively.
- **Updates**: Regularly update your app to add new features and improve performance.

3. Privacy Policy

If your app collects user data, you must have a privacy policy in place and provide a link to it on your app's Play Store listing. Ensure that your privacy policy clearly explains what data you collect and how you use it.

4. Compliance with Google Play Policies

Review and adhere to Google Play's developer policies to avoid app rejections or removal from the Play Store. Common policy violations include:

- **Malicious Behavior**: Apps that harm users' devices or steal their data.
- **Inappropriate Content**: Apps with explicit content or hate speech.
- **Copyright Violations**: Unauthorized use of copyrighted material.
- **Deceptive Practices**: Misleading users or encouraging fraudulent activities.

5. Pricing and Monetization

If your app is paid or offers in-app purchases, set appropriate prices for your products or services. Clearly communicate pricing details to users and provide support for billing issues.

6. Content Rating

Complete the Content Rating questionnaire in the Play Console to assign an appropriate age rating to your app. This ensures that your app is suitable for users of different age groups.

7. Publishing Process

To publish your app on the Play Store, follow these steps:

- **Create a Developer Account**: If you haven't already, create a Google Play Developer account.
- **Prepare Assets**: Gather assets like app icons, screenshots, and promotional materials.
- **Upload Your APK**: Prepare and upload your app's APK file to the Play Console.
- **Fill in App Details**: Complete the Play Store listing with descriptions, screenshots, and other details.
- **Set Pricing and Distribution**: Define your app's pricing, availability, and distribution settings.
- **Testing**: Test your app using the Play Console's internal testing and alpha/beta testing features.
- **Content Rating**: Complete the Content Rating questionnaire.
- **Review and Publish**: Submit your app for review, and once approved, publish it on the Play Store.

8. App Updates

Regularly update your app to fix bugs, add new features, and improve performance. Communicate updates to users through release notes.

9. Marketing and Promotion

Promote your app to increase its visibility and user base. Use social media, online advertising, and other marketing channels to reach a broader audience.

10. User Support and Feedback

Provide user support through email or a dedicated support system. Listen to user feedback and address issues promptly to maintain a positive app reputation.

11. Monitor App Performance

After publishing, monitor your app's performance using the Play Console's analytics tools. Track user engagement, crashes, and revenue to make data-driven improvements.

By following these steps, you can successfully prepare your Android app for the Play Store, reach a wider audience, and provide a great user experience. Remember that maintaining and updating your app is an ongoing process to keep it relevant and competitive in the app marketplace.

Section 15.5: App Distribution and Marketing

Once your Android app is published on the Google Play Store, it's essential to focus on app distribution and marketing strategies to reach a wider audience and maximize its success. Effective distribution and marketing can significantly impact your app's visibility, downloads, and user engagement. In this section, we'll explore various strategies and best practices for app distribution and marketing.

1. App Store Optimization (ASO)

App Store Optimization is the process of improving your app's visibility within the app store's search results. Key ASO strategies include:

- **Keyword Research**: Identify relevant keywords that users might use to search for apps like yours.
- **App Title**: Choose a clear and memorable title that includes relevant keywords.
- **App Description**: Write a compelling and informative description that highlights your app's key features and benefits.
- **Screenshots and Videos**: Use eye-catching visuals to showcase your app's user interface and functionality.
- **Ratings and Reviews**: Encourage users to rate and review your app positively.
- **Localization**: Offer your app in multiple languages to reach a global audience.

2. Social Media Marketing

Utilize social media platforms like Facebook, Twitter, Instagram, and LinkedIn to create awareness and engage with your audience. Share updates, user stories, and promotional content to maintain an active online presence.

3. Content Marketing

Create valuable and informative content related to your app's niche. Blog posts, articles, tutorials, and videos can help establish your authority in your app's domain and attract potential users.

4. Influencer Marketing

Collaborate with influencers in your app's niche to promote your app. Influencers can reach a broad and engaged audience, leading to increased app downloads.

5. Email Marketing

Build an email list of users interested in your app's updates and promotions. Send regular newsletters with valuable content and app-related news to keep users engaged.

6. Paid Advertising

Consider investing in paid advertising campaigns, such as Google Ads, Facebook Ads, or app install ads within other apps. These campaigns can boost your app's visibility and attract users.

7. App Website

Create a dedicated website for your app to provide detailed information, support resources, and contact options for users. A well-designed website can increase credibility and trust.

8. App Updates and Engagement

Frequent app updates that introduce new features or improvements can re-engage existing users and attract new ones. Encourage users to enable notifications to stay informed about updates.

9. User Feedback and Support

Maintain excellent customer support by addressing user feedback and inquiries promptly. Satisfied users are more likely to recommend your app to others.

10. User Referral Programs

Implement referral programs that reward users for referring friends and family to download and use your app. Incentives can include discounts, premium features, or virtual currency.

11. App Analytics

Use app analytics tools to track user behavior, demographics, and engagement metrics. Analyze this data to make informed decisions and optimize your marketing efforts.

12. Community Building

Create a community around your app by establishing forums, social media groups, or chat channels where users can discuss the app, share tips, and provide support to each other.

13. App Store Ad Campaigns

Consider running ad campaigns within the app stores to promote your app. These campaigns can be effective in increasing app downloads, especially during specific promotional periods.

14. App Awards and Recognitions

Submit your app for relevant awards and recognitions within your industry. Winning or being nominated can boost your app's credibility and visibility.

Remember that effective app distribution and marketing are ongoing efforts. Continuously analyze your strategies, adapt to changing trends, and iterate based on user feedback to ensure the long-term success of your Android app. Building a loyal user base and maintaining a positive app reputation are key to sustained growth and success in the competitive app market.

Chapter 16: App Security and Privacy

Section 16.1: Understanding Android Security

Security and privacy are paramount considerations when developing Android apps. Users trust app developers with their data and expect their information to remain confidential and protected. In this section, we will explore the fundamentals of Android security and understand the key aspects that developers should be aware of.

Android Security Architecture

Android provides a multi-layered security architecture to protect user data and the device itself. Here are the primary layers of Android security:

1. **Linux Kernel**: Android is built on top of the Linux kernel, which provides core security features such as process isolation, user privilege separation, and hardware abstraction. This forms the foundation of Android's security model.

2. **Hardware Security**: Modern Android devices come equipped with various hardware security features, including Trusted Execution Environments (TEE), hardware-backed keystore, and biometric authentication (fingerprint, face recognition). These hardware components enhance security by protecting sensitive data and operations.

3. **Application Sandbox**: Android apps run in isolated sandboxes, which means they have limited access to the system and other apps' data. The Android OS enforces strict permission controls to regulate an app's access to device resources and user data.

4. **Permissions Model**: Android uses a permission-based model that requires apps to declare the permissions they need in their manifest files. Users grant or deny these permissions when installing the app, allowing them to control what data and resources the app can access.

5. **Code Signing**: Android apps must be signed with digital certificates. Code signing ensures the integrity and authenticity of the app. Users can verify the app's source and identify any tampering attempts.

6. **Google Play Protect**: Google Play Protect is a built-in security feature that scans apps for malware and harmful behavior. It continuously monitors apps on the device to keep users safe.

7. **Updates and Patching**: Android regularly releases security patches to address known vulnerabilities. Developers should keep their apps up to date and encourage users to update their devices to the latest Android version.

8. **Network Security**: Apps often communicate over networks. Android provides tools and libraries to ensure secure network connections, including HTTPS for web communication and VPN support for secure data transfer.

9. **App Permissions**: Developers should follow the principle of least privilege, meaning apps should request only the permissions they absolutely need. Unnecessary permissions can be a security and privacy risk.

10. **Data Encryption**: Sensitive data should be stored and transmitted securely. Android offers encryption features, and developers should use them to protect user data at rest and in transit.

11. **User Authentication**: Apps that handle user accounts or sensitive data should implement robust user authentication mechanisms. This may include password protection, biometrics, or two-factor authentication.

12. **Privacy Considerations**: Respect user privacy by minimizing data collection and providing transparent privacy policies. Apps should not misuse user data or engage in intrusive tracking without user consent.

13. **Security Testing**: Regularly test your app for security vulnerabilities. Automated tools and manual testing can help identify and fix potential issues before they can be exploited.

By understanding these fundamental aspects of Android security, developers can take the necessary steps to build secure and trustworthy apps. Security is an ongoing process, and developers should stay informed about emerging threats and best practices to protect their users and maintain their app's reputation.

Section 16.2: Implementing App Permissions

App permissions are a critical aspect of Android security and privacy. They define what actions or resources an app can access on a user's device. Properly managing permissions is essential to ensure that your app functions correctly while respecting user privacy and security.

Declaring Permissions

To declare the permissions your app needs, you must include them in the app's AndroidManifest.xml file. You can do this using the `<uses-permission>` element. For example, to request permission to access the device's camera, you would add the following line to your manifest:

```
<uses-permission android:name="android.permission.CAMERA" />
```

Android provides a wide range of permissions for various resources, including the camera, microphone, location, contacts, and more. You should only request the permissions necessary for your app's functionality to minimize the potential for misuse.

Runtime Permission Request

Starting with Android 6.0 (API level 23), apps must request certain permissions at runtime, even if they are declared in the manifest. This change was made to give users more control over app permissions. Here's how you can request permissions at runtime:

1. **Check Permission Status**: Before accessing a resource that requires a permission, check if the permission has been granted using the checkSelfPermission method. For example, to check if you have the CAMERA permission:

```
if (ContextCompat.checkSelfPermission(this, Manifest.permission.CAMERA)
== PackageManager.PERMISSION_GRANTED) {
    // Permission is already granted; proceed with accessing the camera
.
} else {
    // Permission is not granted; request it from the user.
    ActivityCompat.requestPermissions(this, new String[]{Manifest.permi
ssion.CAMERA}, CAMERA_PERMISSION_REQUEST);
}
```

2. **Handle User Response**: After requesting a permission, the user will be prompted to grant or deny it. You must override the onRequestPermissionsResult method to handle the user's response:

```
@Override
public void onRequestPermissionsResult(int requestCode, String[] permis
sions, int[] grantResults) {
        if (requestCode == CAMERA_PERMISSION_REQUEST) {
            if (grantResults.length > 0 && grantResults[0] == PackageManage
r.PERMISSION_GRANTED) {
                // Permission granted; proceed with accessing the camera.
            } else {
                // Permission denied; handle accordingly (e.g., inform the
user).
            }
        }
}
```

3. **Explain Why**: When requesting permissions, it's essential to explain to the user why your app needs them. You can use the shouldShowRequestPermissionRationale method to check if you should show an explanation:

```
if (ActivityCompat.shouldShowRequestPermissionRationale(this, Manifest.
permission.CAMERA)) {
    // Show an explanation to the user.
}
```

4. **Request Multiple Permissions**: If your app requires multiple permissions, you can request them simultaneously:

```
ActivityCompat.requestPermissions(this,
    new String[]{Manifest.permission.CAMERA, Manifest.permission.READ_C
ONTACTS},
    MULTIPLE_PERMISSIONS_REQUEST);
```

Here are some best practices for handling app permissions:

- Request permissions only when needed: Avoid requesting permissions that your app doesn't immediately require. Request them when the user initiates an action that requires the permission.

- Explain the purpose: Clearly explain why your app needs a particular permission. Users are more likely to grant permissions if they understand the purpose.

- Handle permission denials gracefully: Your app should gracefully handle scenarios where users deny permissions. Provide alternative ways to use the app's core features.

- Check for permission changes: Users can change app permissions at any time in the device settings. Check for permission status before accessing resources and respond accordingly.

- Keep up with best practices: Android's permission system may evolve with updates. Stay informed about the latest best practices and changes in permission handling.

By following these guidelines, you can implement effective and user-friendly permission management in your Android app, enhancing both security and user trust.

Section 16.3: Data Encryption and Protection

Data security is a paramount concern in Android app development. Protecting sensitive user data, such as login credentials or personal information, is not only a best practice but also a legal requirement in many regions. Data encryption is a fundamental technique to ensure the confidentiality and integrity of data stored on a device.

Encryption Basics

Encryption is the process of converting data into a secure, unreadable format that can only be accessed with the appropriate decryption key. Android provides robust encryption APIs to secure data at rest.

Android Keystore

The Android Keystore is a system-level cryptographic library that stores sensitive information like cryptographic keys in a secure container. Keys stored in the Keystore are protected against various attacks, including extraction by malicious apps.

To create and use keys in the Android Keystore, you typically use the `KeyStore` and `KeyGenerator` classes:

```
KeyStore keyStore = KeyStore.getInstance("AndroidKeyStore");
keyStore.load(null);

KeyGenerator keyGenerator = KeyGenerator.getInstance(KeyProperties.KEY_ALGORI
THM_AES, "AndroidKeyStore");
KeyGenParameterSpec keySpec = new KeyGenParameterSpec.Builder(KEY_ALIAS, KeyP
roperties.PURPOSE_ENCRYPT | KeyProperties.PURPOSE_DECRYPT)
    .setBlockModes(KeyProperties.BLOCK_MODE_CBC)
    .setEncryptionPaddings(KeyProperties.ENCRYPTION_PADDING_PKCS7)
    .setUserAuthenticationRequired(true) // Optionally, require user authenti
cation
    .build();
keyGenerator.init(keySpec);
SecretKey secretKey = keyGenerator.generateKey();
```

Encrypting Data

Once you have a cryptographic key, you can use it to encrypt and decrypt data. For example, to encrypt a sensitive string:

```
Cipher cipher = Cipher.getInstance("AES/CBC/PKCS7Padding");
cipher.init(Cipher.ENCRYPT_MODE, secretKey);

byte[] encryptedData = cipher.doFinal(data.getBytes());
```

Decryption

Decryption works similarly, using the same key and the appropriate decryption mode:

```
cipher.init(Cipher.DECRYPT_MODE, secretKey);
byte[] decryptedData = cipher.doFinal(encryptedData);
String originalData = new String(decryptedData);
```

SharedPreferences Encryption

If your app stores sensitive data in SharedPreferences, it's crucial to encrypt it to prevent unauthorized access. You can create a custom SharedPreferences implementation that encrypts and decrypts data transparently.

Here's a simplified example of an encrypted SharedPreferences class:

```
public class EncryptedSharedPreferences {
    private SharedPreferences sharedPreferences;
```

```java
    private Cipher encryptionCipher;
    private Cipher decryptionCipher;

    public EncryptedSharedPreferences(Context context) throws Exception {
        sharedPreferences = context.getSharedPreferences("encrypted_prefs", C
ontext.MODE_PRIVATE);
        encryptionCipher = Cipher.getInstance("AES/CBC/PKCS7Padding");
        decryptionCipher = Cipher.getInstance("AES/CBC/PKCS7Padding");
        // Initialize ciphers with the appropriate keys and IVs
        // ...

        // Optionally, use the Android Keystore to securely store and retriev
e keys
        // ...
    }

    public void putString(String key, String value) {
        byte[] encryptedData = encrypt(value);
        String encodedData = Base64.encodeToString(encryptedData, Base64.DEFA
ULT);
        sharedPreferences.edit().putString(key, encodedData).apply();
    }

    public String getString(String key, String defaultValue) {
        String encodedData = sharedPreferences.getString(key, null);
        if (encodedData != null) {
            byte[] encryptedData = Base64.decode(encodedData, Base64.DEFAULT)
;

            return decrypt(encryptedData);
        }
        return defaultValue;
    }

    private byte[] encrypt(String data) {
        // Encrypt data using the encryptionCipher
        // ...
    }

    private String decrypt(byte[] encryptedData) {
        // Decrypt data using the decryptionCipher
        // ...
    }
}
```

Security Considerations

- **Key Management**: Safeguard cryptographic keys, as they are crucial for encryption. Consider using the Android Keystore for key storage.

- **User Authentication**: Depending on your app's sensitivity, require user authentication before granting access to encrypted data.

- **Algorithm and Mode**: Choose strong encryption algorithms and modes. AES with CBC and PKCS7Padding is a common choice.

- **Secure Storage**: Ensure that encrypted data is stored securely. Avoid storing encryption keys alongside encrypted data.

By implementing robust encryption practices, you can protect sensitive user data and enhance the security of your Android app. However, encryption is just one aspect of overall app security, so a comprehensive security strategy is recommended.

Section 16.4: Securing Network Communications

Securing network communications is essential for protecting sensitive data transferred between your Android app and remote servers or services. Without proper security measures, data transmitted over the network can be intercepted or tampered with. This section explores common practices for securing network communications in Android apps.

1. Use HTTPS

When your app communicates with a server, always use HTTPS (HTTP Secure) instead of HTTP. HTTPS encrypts data in transit, making it difficult for attackers to eavesdrop on the communication.

You can use libraries like OkHttp to make secure network requests:

```
OkHttpClient client = new OkHttpClient.Builder()
    .sslSocketFactory(sslContext.getSocketFactory(), trustManager)
    .build();

Request request = new Request.Builder()
    .url("https://example.com/api/resource")
    .build();

try {
    Response response = client.newCall(request).execute();
    // Handle the response
} catch (IOException e) {
    // Handle network errors
}
```

2. Certificate Pinning

Certificate pinning enhances security by associating a specific SSL/TLS certificate with the remote server. This prevents man-in-the-middle attacks, where attackers replace the server's certificate with a malicious one.

```java
CertificatePinner certificatePinner = new CertificatePinner.Builder()
    .add("example.com", "sha256/AAAAAAAAAAAAAAAAAAAAAAAAAAAAAAA=")
    .build();

OkHttpClient client = new OkHttpClient.Builder()
    .certificatePinner(certificatePinner)
    .build();
```

3. Network Security Configuration

Android allows you to specify network security configurations in your app's manifest. These configurations define security requirements for network connections, including trust anchors (CA certificates) and domains.

```xml
<!-- res/xml/network_security_config.xml -->
<network-security-config>
    <domain-config cleartextTrafficPermitted="false">
        <domain includeSubdomains="true">example.com</domain>
        <trust-anchors>
            <certificates src="@raw/my_ca_cert"/>
        </trust-anchors>
    </domain-config>
</network-security-config>
```

In the above example, we enforce that connections to "example.com" must use HTTPS, and we specify a custom CA certificate.

4. OAuth and API Keys

When accessing third-party APIs, use OAuth for authentication and authorization. Never embed API keys directly in your app's code or resources, as they can be extracted by attackers.

5. Data Encryption

If your app exchanges sensitive data with a server, consider encrypting the data before transmission and decrypting it on the server side. This adds an extra layer of security to protect data during transit.

6. Input Validation and Sanitization

Validate and sanitize user inputs before sending them to a server. Input validation prevents attackers from injecting malicious code or conducting injection attacks like SQL injection.

7. Secure Data Transmission

Use secure protocols and libraries for data transmission. Libraries like TLS/SSL and tools like Wireshark can help ensure secure data exchange.

8. Security Testing

Regularly test your app's network security using tools like OWASP ZAP or Burp Suite. Conduct penetration testing to identify vulnerabilities and address them promptly.

By implementing these network security practices, you can significantly reduce the risk of data breaches and enhance the overall security of your Android app. Remember that security is an ongoing process, and staying informed about the latest security threats and best practices is crucial.

Section 16.5: Privacy Policy and Compliance

Privacy is a paramount concern when developing Android apps, and it's essential to comply with various privacy laws and regulations, such as the General Data Protection Regulation (GDPR) and the California Consumer Privacy Act (CCPA). This section discusses the importance of privacy policies, compliance considerations, and best practices.

1. Privacy Policy

A privacy policy is a legal document that informs users about how your app collects, uses, and safeguards their data. It's a critical component of app development, and many app stores, including Google Play Store and Apple App Store, require developers to provide a link to their privacy policy.

In your privacy policy, you should:

- Clearly explain what data your app collects and why.
- Describe how user data is stored and secured.
- Inform users about their rights and how to exercise them.
- Provide contact information for privacy-related inquiries.

2. User Consent

Obtaining user consent is crucial when collecting personal data. Android provides the `android.permission.READ_PHONE_STATE` permission as an example. If your app needs access to sensitive information like the user's phone state, you must request the user's permission at runtime.

```
if (ContextCompat.checkSelfPermission(this, Manifest.permission.READ_PHONE_ST
ATE)
        != PackageManager.PERMISSION_GRANTED) {
    // Permission is not granted, request it.
    ActivityCompat.requestPermissions(this,
            new String[]{Manifest.permission.READ_PHONE_STATE},
            MY_PERMISSIONS_REQUEST_READ_PHONE_STATE);
}
```

3. Data Minimization

Collect only the data that your app needs to function. Avoid collecting excessive or unnecessary data that can compromise user privacy. Data minimization is a fundamental principle of privacy by design.

4. Data Encryption

Encrypt sensitive data both in transit and at rest. Android provides APIs for data encryption, including the Android Keystore for secure storage of cryptographic keys.

5. Third-Party Libraries and SDKs

Review and vet third-party libraries and SDKs used in your app. Some third-party components may collect user data independently, so it's crucial to understand their data handling practices and ensure they align with your privacy policy.

6. Consent Management SDKs

Consider using consent management SDKs that help manage user consents for data collection and processing. These SDKs can simplify compliance with privacy regulations.

7. Regular Audits and Updates

Regularly review and update your app's privacy practices to stay compliant with evolving privacy laws. Conduct audits to ensure your app adheres to its privacy policy and regulations.

8. Compliance with GDPR, CCPA, and Others

If your app is available to users in regions like the European Union (EU) or California, ensure compliance with GDPR and CCPA. This may involve providing mechanisms for users to access, delete, or export their data.

9. Educate Your Team

Make sure your development team is aware of privacy best practices. Training and awareness programs can help prevent accidental privacy violations.

10. Privacy by Design

Incorporate privacy considerations into the early stages of app development. Privacy by design ensures that privacy is an integral part of your app's architecture and functionality.

Remember that privacy is not just a legal requirement but also a fundamental aspect of building trust with your users. Prioritizing user privacy can lead to increased user confidence and a better reputation for your app.

In summary, safeguarding user privacy is a shared responsibility between developers and users. By adopting privacy best practices and complying with relevant regulations, you can protect user data and build trust in your Android app.

Chapter 17: Testing and Debugging Your App

Section 17.1: Unit Testing in Android

Unit testing is a fundamental aspect of Android app development that helps ensure the reliability and correctness of your code. It involves testing individual components or units of your app's code in isolation. In this section, we'll explore the importance of unit testing in Android development, how to set up and write unit tests, and some best practices.

Why Unit Testing?

Unit testing offers several benefits in Android app development:

1. **Bug Detection**: It helps identify and fix bugs early in the development process, reducing the cost of bug fixing later.

2. **Regression Testing**: Unit tests ensure that existing functionality remains intact when you make changes to your code.

3. **Code Quality**: Writing testable code often leads to cleaner, modular, and maintainable code.

4. **Documentation**: Unit tests serve as living documentation for your code, illustrating how it should behave.

Setting Up Unit Testing

Android provides a testing framework called JUnit for writing unit tests. To set up unit testing in your Android project, follow these steps:

1. **Add Dependencies**: Open your app-level `build.gradle` file and add the following dependencies:

```
dependencies {
    testImplementation 'junit:junit:4.13.2'
}
```

2. **Create a Test Folder**: In your project's directory structure, create a folder named `test` under the `src` folder (e.g., `src/test/java/com/example/myapp/`).

3. **Write Test Classes**: Create test classes that mirror your app's package structure and add test methods within these classes.

Writing Unit Tests

Let's look at an example of a simple unit test for a hypothetical `Calculator` class:

```
import org.junit.Test;
import static org.junit.Assert.*;
```

```java
public class CalculatorTest {

    @Test
    public void addition_isCorrect() {
        Calculator calculator = new Calculator();
        int result = calculator.add(2, 3);
        assertEquals(5, result);
    }
}
```

In this test:

- We import the necessary JUnit classes.
- We create a test method, `addition_isCorrect`, that tests the `add` method of the `Calculator` class.
- Inside the test method, we create an instance of the `Calculator` class, perform an addition operation, and assert that the result is as expected.

Running Unit Tests

To run unit tests in Android Studio:

1. Right-click on the test class or method.
2. Select "Run" or "Debug."

Android Studio will execute the tests and provide feedback on whether they pass or fail.

Best Practices for Unit Testing

Here are some best practices to follow when writing unit tests for your Android app:

1. **Test Only One Thing**: Each unit test should focus on testing a single piece of functionality.

2. **Isolate Dependencies**: Use mocking frameworks like Mockito to isolate dependencies and test the unit in isolation.

3. **Keep Tests Fast**: Unit tests should execute quickly. Slow tests can hinder the development process.

4. **Test Edge Cases**: Ensure that your tests cover edge cases and boundary conditions.

5. **Use Descriptive Names**: Name your test methods descriptively to indicate what is being tested.

6. **Regularly Run Tests**: Run your tests frequently to catch issues early.

7. **Refactor Tests**: Refactor your tests as your code evolves to keep them relevant.

8. **Continuous Integration**: Integrate unit tests into your CI/CD pipeline for automated testing.

Unit testing is an essential practice for building robust and reliable Android apps. By following best practices and incorporating unit tests into your development workflow, you can catch bugs early, improve code quality, and make your app more maintainable.

Section 17.2: Debugging Techniques and Tools

Debugging is an indispensable skill for Android developers, allowing you to identify and fix issues in your app's code. In this section, we'll explore various debugging techniques and tools available for Android development.

1. Logcat:

Logcat is a crucial debugging tool that allows you to view logs generated by your app. You can use Log class methods to write log messages in your code and then view them in the Logcat tab of Android Studio. Common log levels include Log.d (debug), Log.i (information), Log.w (warning), and Log.e (error). Example:

```
Log.d("TAG", "This is a debug message.");
```

2. Breakpoints:

Breakpoints are markers that you can place in your code to pause program execution at specific points. You can inspect variables, step through code, and identify issues step by step. To set a breakpoint, click on the left margin of your code editor in Android Studio.

3. Debugger:

Android Studio comes with a built-in debugger. You can start debugging by clicking the "Debug" button or pressing Shift + F9. The debugger allows you to step through your code, inspect variables, evaluate expressions, and set watches.

4. Inspecting Variables:

While debugging, you can hover over variables in your code to see their current values. Android Studio also provides a "Variables" tab where you can inspect and modify variable values during debugging.

5. Evaluate Expressions:

You can evaluate expressions in the "Evaluate Expression" window while debugging. This is helpful for checking values and performing calculations during debugging sessions.

6. Profiling Tools:

Android Profiler is a suite of tools for profiling your app's performance. It includes CPU, Memory, and Network profilers. These tools help you identify performance bottlenecks and memory leaks.

7. Crash Reports:

Services like Firebase Crashlytics can provide detailed crash reports when your app crashes in the wild. These reports help you quickly identify and fix issues experienced by users.

8. MonkeyRunner:

MonkeyRunner is a tool for running automated tests and generating events in the emulator or on physical devices. It's useful for testing the UI and simulating user interactions.

9. Third-Party Libraries:

There are third-party debugging libraries like Stetho and Flipper that provide advanced debugging capabilities. Stetho, for example, allows you to inspect your app's network traffic and databases.

10. Remote Debugging:

You can debug your app on a physical device remotely using ADB (Android Debug Bridge). This is valuable for debugging issues that only occur on specific devices.

11. Lint Checks:

Android Studio includes Lint, a static analysis tool that checks your code for potential issues. Running lint checks can help you catch problems early.

12. Version Control:

Using version control systems like Git, you can track changes to your code, collaborate with others, and easily revert to previous versions if issues arise.

Debugging is an iterative process that requires patience and a systematic approach. By using these debugging techniques and tools effectively, you can pinpoint and resolve issues in your Android app, ensuring a smoother user experience and higher app quality.

Section 17.3: Profiling and Performance Optimization

Performance optimization is a critical aspect of Android app development. Users expect apps to be fast and responsive, and optimizing your app's performance can lead to better user satisfaction and retention. In this section, we'll explore profiling and performance optimization techniques for Android apps.

Profiling involves analyzing your app's behavior and identifying performance bottlenecks. Android Studio provides a set of profiling tools to help you with this task:

- **CPU Profiler**: This tool allows you to monitor CPU usage and identify CPU-intensive operations in your app. You can see how much time your app spends in various methods and functions.

- **Memory Profiler**: Memory leaks and excessive memory usage can lead to app crashes and sluggish performance. The Memory Profiler helps you track memory allocation and deallocation, find memory leaks, and optimize memory usage.

- **Network Profiler**: If your app relies on network requests, the Network Profiler helps you monitor network activity, including requests and responses. It can reveal issues like excessive network traffic or slow network requests.

- **GPU Profiler**: For graphics-intensive apps or games, the GPU Profiler can be invaluable. It provides insights into your app's rendering performance, including frame rendering times and GPU usage.

2. Optimizing Your Code:

Once you've identified performance bottlenecks using profiling tools, it's time to optimize your code:

- **Algorithmic Optimization**: Review your code's algorithms and data structures. Sometimes, a more efficient algorithm can significantly improve performance.

- **Avoiding Redundant Work**: Look for areas where your app performs redundant calculations or operations. Caching or memoization can help eliminate unnecessary work.

- **Background Processing**: Move resource-intensive tasks to background threads or use asynchronous techniques like coroutines (Kotlin) or AsyncTask (Java) to prevent blocking the main UI thread.

- **Optimizing Layouts**: Complex layouts can slow down your app. Use the Hierarchy Viewer to inspect your layout hierarchy and flatten layouts where possible.

3. Reducing APK Size:

Large APK sizes can lead to slower app installation and increased storage usage on users' devices. To reduce APK size:

- **Use Android App Bundles**: Publish your app using the Android App Bundle format, which allows Google Play to generate optimized APKs for each user's device, reducing unnecessary resources.

- **Resource Shrinking**: Enable resource shrinking to remove unused resources from your APK. Proguard (for Java) or R8 (for Kotlin) can also help remove unused code.

- **Image Compression**: Compress images and use modern image formats like WebP to reduce the size of image assets.

4. Network Optimization:

For apps that rely on network requests:

- **Use Caching**: Implement caching mechanisms to store frequently accessed data locally. This reduces the need for frequent network requests.

- **Batching Requests**: Combine multiple network requests into a single request to minimize overhead.

- **Reduce Payload Size**: Minimize the data transferred between the app and the server by using efficient data formats like Protocol Buffers or JSON with compression.

5. Testing and Benchmarking:

Regularly test your app's performance on various devices and under different conditions. Benchmarking tools can help you measure improvements and identify regressions.

6. Battery Optimization:

Optimizing for battery life is essential. Avoid continuous background processes, excessive wake locks, and frequent GPS or sensor polling, as these can drain the battery quickly.

By profiling your app, optimizing your code, reducing APK size, optimizing network usage, testing, and considering battery impact, you can create Android apps that are not only feature-rich but also deliver an excellent user experience with optimal performance.

Section 17.4: Beta Testing and Feedback

Beta testing is a crucial phase in the development of an Android app. It allows you to gather feedback from real users before releasing your app to a wider audience. In this section, we'll explore the importance of beta testing, how to set up beta tests, and strategies for collecting valuable user feedback.

1. Why Beta Testing Matters:

Beta testing provides several benefits:

- **Bug Detection**: Real users can uncover bugs and issues that you might have missed during development and testing.

- **Usability Feedback**: Beta testers can provide insights into the user experience, helping you identify usability problems and areas for improvement.

- **Device and OS Diversity**: Beta testing allows you to evaluate your app's performance on a variety of devices and Android versions.

- **Feature Validation**: You can validate whether your app's features meet user expectations and needs.

2. Setting Up Beta Tests:

Here's how to set up beta tests for your Android app:

- **Google Play Console**: Use the Google Play Console to manage beta testing. You can create a closed beta, open beta, or internal test track.

- **Closed Beta**: Invite a select group of users to test your app. You can use email addresses or Google Groups to manage access.

- **Open Beta**: Make your app available for anyone to join the beta test. This option is suitable for gathering a larger user base.

- **Internal Testing**: Use the internal test track to test your app with your development team before releasing it to external beta testers.

3. Collecting Feedback:

Collecting feedback from beta testers is essential. Here are some strategies:

- **Feedback Channels**: Provide clear channels for users to submit feedback, such as in-app feedback forms, email, or dedicated forums.

- **Feedback Categories**: Categorize feedback into areas like bugs, usability issues, feature requests, and performance problems.

- **Regular Updates**: Keep your beta testers informed about updates and changes based on their feedback.

- **Feedback Analysis**: Analyze the feedback and prioritize issues based on severity and impact on the user experience.

4. Iterative Development:

Use the feedback from beta testers to iterate on your app. Fix reported bugs, address usability issues, and consider feature requests that align with your app's goals.

5. Monitoring and Analytics:

Integrate analytics tools into your app to gather data on user behavior. Track crashes, user engagement, and user flows to identify areas for improvement.

Maintain open and transparent communication with your beta testers. Acknowledge their contributions and show them that their feedback is valued.

7. Privacy and Data Handling:

Ensure that you handle user data responsibly and comply with privacy regulations. Inform users about data collection and usage in your app.

8. Release Planning:

Once you've addressed feedback and are confident in your app's stability and usability, plan for the official release. Consider staggered rollouts to monitor the app's performance with a broader audience.

In conclusion, beta testing is a vital part of the app development lifecycle. It helps you identify and resolve issues, improve user experience, and ensure your app works effectively on a variety of devices and Android versions. Embrace feedback from beta testers as a valuable resource for making your app successful in the competitive Android marketplace.

Section 17.5: Continuous Integration and Deployment

Continuous Integration (CI) and Continuous Deployment (CD) are essential practices in modern Android app development. They streamline the process of building, testing, and deploying your app, ensuring that it remains reliable and up-to-date throughout its lifecycle. In this section, we'll explore the concepts of CI/CD for Android and how to set up an effective CI/CD pipeline.

1. Understanding CI/CD:

- **Continuous Integration (CI)**: CI involves automatically building and testing your app's code whenever changes are made to the version control repository (e.g., Git). This ensures that new code doesn't introduce bugs or break existing functionality.

- **Continuous Deployment (CD)**: CD takes CI a step further by automating the deployment process. When new code passes CI tests, it can be automatically deployed to a staging or production environment, making it available to users.

2. Benefits of CI/CD:

Implementing CI/CD in your Android app development workflow offers several advantages:

- **Early Bug Detection**: CI detects issues as soon as code changes are committed, reducing the chances of introducing bugs.

- **Faster Development**: Automation speeds up the build, test, and deployment processes, allowing for faster development cycles.

- **Consistency**: CI/CD ensures that builds and deployments are consistent, reducing the "it works on my machine" problem.

- **Reliability**: Automated tests and deployments improve the overall reliability of your app.

3. Setting Up CI/CD for Android:

To set up CI/CD for your Android project, follow these steps:

- **Choose a CI/CD Service**: There are various CI/CD services available, such as Jenkins, Travis CI, CircleCI, and GitHub Actions. Select one that suits your needs.

- **Configure Build Environment**: Specify the build environment for your Android project, including the Android SDK, Gradle, and required dependencies.

- **Version Control Integration**: Connect your CI/CD service to your version control repository (e.g., GitHub, GitLab). Configure webhooks or triggers to start CI builds automatically on code changes.

- **Define CI Workflow**: Create a CI workflow that includes building the app, running tests (unit tests and UI tests), and generating artifacts.

- **Artifact Storage**: Store build artifacts, such as APK files, in a secure location accessible to your CD pipeline.

- **Implement Deployment Steps**: For CD, define the deployment steps, including staging and production deployments. Ensure proper testing in staging environments.

- **Monitoring and Alerts**: Set up monitoring and alerts to be notified of build or deployment failures.

4. CI/CD Best Practices:

- **Automated Testing**: Implement a robust suite of automated tests, including unit tests and UI tests, to catch regressions early.

- **Immutable Builds**: Ensure that builds are reproducible and use immutable build environments to eliminate inconsistencies.

- **Rollback Mechanism**: Implement a rollback mechanism in your CD pipeline to revert to a previous version in case of issues.

- **Security Scanning**: Include security scans in your CI/CD pipeline to identify vulnerabilities in your app.

- **Documentation**: Maintain clear documentation for your CI/CD setup, including build and deployment scripts.

- **Collaboration**: Encourage collaboration between developers, testers, and operations teams to streamline the CI/CD process.

5. Continuous Improvement:

CI/CD is not a one-time setup; it's an ongoing practice. Continuously monitor and improve your CI/CD pipeline to adapt to changing requirements and technologies.

In conclusion, CI/CD is a fundamental practice that enhances the efficiency, reliability, and quality of your Android app development process. By automating builds, tests, and deployments, you can deliver high-quality apps to your users with confidence and agility.

Chapter 18: Building Full-Featured Apps

Section 18.1: Project Planning and Scoping

When it comes to building full-featured Android apps, effective project planning and scoping are crucial. These initial stages lay the foundation for a successful development process. In this section, we'll explore the key aspects of project planning and scoping for Android app development.

1. Define Your App's Purpose and Goals:

Before diving into development, clearly define the purpose and goals of your app. Ask yourself questions like:

- What problem does the app solve?
- Who is the target audience?
- What features are essential?
- What are the desired user interactions?
- What are the project's objectives and success criteria?

Having a well-defined vision helps align the development team and stakeholders.

2. Market Research and Competitor Analysis:

Research the market to understand existing solutions and identify gaps your app can fill. Analyze competitors to learn from their strengths and weaknesses. Market research helps refine your app's unique selling points.

3. User Experience (UX) Design:

Invest time in UX design to create an intuitive and user-friendly interface. Consider user personas, wireframes, and prototypes to visualize the app's flow and layout. UX design enhances user satisfaction and engagement.

4. Functional Requirements:

Document functional requirements that outline what the app should do. Use user stories or use cases to describe interactions from a user's perspective. Prioritize features and create a backlog.

5. Technical Feasibility:

Evaluate the technical feasibility of your app's features. Ensure you have the necessary skills, tools, and technologies. Address potential technical challenges early in the planning phase.

6. Estimate Time and Resources:

Break down the project into tasks and estimate the time required for each. Consider factors like development, testing, and deployment. Allocate resources, including developers, designers, and testers.

7. Budgeting and Cost Analysis:

Create a budget that covers development costs, marketing, and ongoing maintenance. Factor in potential contingencies. A well-planned budget helps prevent financial surprises.

8. Project Timeline:

Create a project timeline that includes milestones, deadlines, and deliverables. Use project management tools like Gantt charts or agile methodologies like Scrum or Kanban for effective project tracking.

9. Risk Assessment and Mitigation:

Identify potential risks and develop mitigation strategies. Risks could include technical challenges, changing market conditions, or unexpected delays. Having a risk management plan in place helps maintain project stability.

10. Legal and Compliance Considerations:

Understand legal aspects, such as data privacy regulations (e.g., GDPR), intellectual property rights, and licensing requirements. Ensure your app complies with relevant laws and standards.

11. Testing and Quality Assurance:

Include testing and quality assurance processes in your project plan. Define testing scenarios, criteria for success, and regression testing strategies. Quality assurance is vital for delivering a bug-free app.

12. Documentation:

Maintain thorough documentation throughout the project. Document requirements, design decisions, and technical details. Proper documentation aids in knowledge sharing and future maintenance.

13. Stakeholder Communication:

Establish clear communication channels with stakeholders, including clients, users, and team members. Regular updates and feedback loops help manage expectations.

14. Project Scope Management:

Scope creep, where new features are added without proper assessment, can derail a project. Implement scope management procedures to control changes effectively.

15. Flexibility and Adaptability:

While planning is crucial, be prepared to adapt to changing circumstances. Agile methodologies allow for flexibility, enabling you to respond to evolving requirements.

Effective project planning and scoping set the stage for a successful Android app development journey. By investing time and effort in these initial phases, you increase the likelihood of delivering a high-quality, user-friendly app that meets its goals and delights its users.

Section 18.2: Building a Messaging App

Building a messaging app is a challenging but rewarding endeavor in the realm of Android app development. Messaging apps have become an integral part of modern communication, connecting people across the globe. In this section, we'll explore the key considerations and steps involved in building a messaging app.

1. Concept and Features:

Before diving into development, define the concept and features of your messaging app. Consider features such as real-time messaging, multimedia sharing, group chats, notifications, and encryption for security.

2. Choosing a Backend Solution:

Messaging apps often require a robust backend infrastructure to handle real-time communication. Consider using technologies like Firebase Realtime Database, MQTT, or WebSocket for real-time messaging capabilities.

3. User Authentication:

Implement user authentication to ensure that only registered users can access the messaging platform. Common authentication methods include email/password, phone number verification, or third-party social media authentication.

4. Real-Time Messaging:

Implement real-time messaging functionality using technologies like Firebase Cloud Messaging (FCM) or WebSocket. Messages should be delivered instantly, and users should be able to see when their messages are read (read receipts).

5. Multimedia Sharing:

Enable users to share images, videos, audio, and other multimedia files within the chat. Implement media upload/download functionality and ensure that multimedia files are compressed to save bandwidth.

6. Group Chats:

Allow users to create and participate in group chats. Implement features like group creation, member management, and group-specific settings.

7. Notifications:

Implement push notifications to alert users about new messages, even when the app is not open. Ensure that notifications are customizable, allowing users to mute specific chats or customize notification tones.

8. Security and Encryption:

Messaging apps should prioritize user data security. Implement end-to-end encryption to protect message content from unauthorized access. Consider using established encryption libraries like Signal Protocol.

9. Offline Messaging:

Allow users to send messages even when they are offline. Implement a mechanism to store and deliver messages once the recipient comes online.

10. Search and Navigation:

Implement search functionality to help users find specific messages or chats quickly. Create an intuitive navigation system that allows users to switch between chats effortlessly.

11. Sync Across Devices:

Enable users to access their chats and messages from multiple devices. Implement synchronization mechanisms to keep messages up-to-date across platforms.

12. User Profile Management:

Allow users to set up profiles, including profile pictures and status messages. Implement privacy settings to control who can view their profile information.

13. Reporting and Moderation:

To maintain a healthy community, implement reporting and moderation features. Users should be able to report inappropriate content or users, and moderators should have tools to manage reported content.

14. Testing and Performance Optimization:

Thoroughly test the app to ensure that it performs well under various conditions, especially in scenarios with a high volume of messages and users. Optimize performance and address memory and battery consumption issues.

15. Compliance and Regulations:

Be aware of data privacy regulations and ensure that your app complies with them. Provide clear terms of service and privacy policies to users.

16. User Feedback and Updates:

Collect user feedback and use it to improve the app. Regularly update the app to fix bugs, add new features, and enhance security.

Building a messaging app is a complex undertaking that requires careful planning and attention to detail. By following these key considerations and best practices, you can create a messaging app that provides a seamless and secure communication experience for your users.

Section 18.3: Creating a Social Media App

Creating a social media app is a substantial undertaking that involves several key considerations. Social media platforms are known for their ability to connect users, share content, and foster online communities. In this section, we'll explore the fundamental aspects of building a social media app.

1. Defining the Concept:

Before you start developing a social media app, you need a clear concept and target audience. Decide on the core functionality and features that will make your app unique. Determine whether it will be a general-purpose platform or focus on a specific niche.

2. User Authentication:

Implement a robust user authentication system. Users should be able to create accounts, log in securely, and recover their passwords. Consider offering social media login options for convenience.

3. User Profiles:

Allow users to create and customize profiles. Users should be able to add profile pictures, bios, and links to their personal websites or social media profiles.

4. Content Sharing:

The core of any social media app is content sharing. Users should be able to create and share text posts, images, videos, and links. Implement features like tagging, mentions, and hashtags for better content discovery.

5. Feed and Timeline:

Design a user-friendly feed or timeline where users can see posts from people they follow or engage with. Implement algorithms for content recommendations and personalization.

6. Likes, Comments, and Shares:

Enable users to interact with posts by liking, commenting, and sharing them. Implement real-time updates to display new interactions.

7. Messaging and Chat:

Implement direct messaging features to enable private conversations between users. Ensure that messages are delivered in real-time and support multimedia sharing.

8. Notifications:

Implement push notifications to keep users informed about likes, comments, mentions, and new followers. Allow users to customize notification preferences.

9. Privacy Settings:

Give users control over their privacy settings. Allow them to choose who can see their posts, send them messages, or follow them. Implement blocking and reporting mechanisms for user safety.

10. Search and Discovery:

Create a powerful search feature that allows users to find other users, posts, or topics of interest. Implement trending sections and explore pages for content discovery.

11. User Engagement:

Encourage user engagement by implementing features like gamification (e.g., badges or rewards), user-generated content challenges, and user-generated content curation.

12. Moderation and Content Filtering:

To maintain a positive and safe environment, implement content moderation tools to detect and remove inappropriate content. Ensure that your app complies with community guidelines and regulations.

13. Analytics and Insights:

Provide users with insights into their activity, such as post views, likes, and follower growth. Offer analytics to help users understand their audience better.

14. Monetization Strategies:

Consider various monetization strategies, such as in-app advertising, sponsored posts, premium subscriptions, or virtual goods. Ensure that your monetization methods align with your users' preferences and expectations.

15. Scaling and Performance:

Design your app with scalability in mind. As your user base grows, your app should be able to handle increased traffic and interactions. Optimize performance to provide a smooth user experience.

16. Testing and Quality Assurance:

Thoroughly test your app to identify and fix bugs, performance issues, and security vulnerabilities. Conduct usability testing to ensure that the user interface is intuitive.

17. Updates and Community Feedback:

Regularly update your app to add new features, improve security, and address user feedback. Maintain an active presence on social media platforms to engage with your user community.

Building a successful social media app requires a deep understanding of user behavior, strong technical skills, and a commitment to maintaining a safe and engaging platform. By following these key considerations, you can create a social media app that attracts and retains users while fostering meaningful online connections.

Section 18.4: Developing a Productivity App

Productivity apps are designed to help users manage their tasks, organize their work, and achieve their goals efficiently. Developing a productivity app requires careful planning and consideration of user needs. In this section, we'll explore the key elements involved in creating a productivity app.

1. Identify the Target Audience:

Before you begin developing your productivity app, identify your target audience. Are you building a task manager for individuals, a project management tool for teams, or a note-taking app for students? Understanding your users' needs is crucial.

2. Define Core Features:

Determine the core features your productivity app will offer. Common features include task creation and management, reminders, calendars, note-taking, goal setting, and file organization. Prioritize features based on their importance and relevance to your target audience.

3. User-Friendly Interface:

Design an intuitive and user-friendly interface. Users should be able to navigate your app easily and access essential features without confusion. Consider using familiar design patterns and providing clear instructions.

4. Task Management:

Implement robust task management capabilities. Users should be able to create, edit, categorize, prioritize, and organize tasks. Allow for due dates, labels, tags, and task completion tracking.

5. Reminders and Notifications:

Include reminders and notifications to help users stay on top of their tasks and deadlines. Ensure that notifications are customizable to suit individual preferences.

6. Calendar Integration:

If applicable, integrate a calendar feature. Users can schedule events, appointments, and deadlines within your app and sync them with their device's calendar.

7. Note-Taking and Document Management:

Implement note-taking functionality. Users should be able to create, edit, and organize notes efficiently. Consider supporting rich text, attachments, and document scanning.

8. Goal Setting and Tracking:

Allow users to set and track their goals. This could include personal, professional, or educational objectives. Provide progress tracking and achievement celebrations.

9. Collaboration and Sharing:

If your app is for teams or collaboration, include features for sharing tasks, projects, and notes. Implement user roles and permissions to control access.

10. Sync and Cloud Storage:

Enable users to sync their data across devices and access it from anywhere. Implement secure cloud storage for data backup and recovery.

11. Offline Access:

Ensure that your app functions offline or in low-connectivity environments. Users should be able to view and edit their tasks and notes even without an internet connection.

12. Search and Filters:

Incorporate a robust search functionality and filters. Users should be able to quickly find tasks, notes, or documents based on keywords, categories, or tags.

13. Security and Privacy:

Prioritize the security of user data. Implement encryption, authentication, and secure access controls. Clearly communicate your app's privacy policy to users.

14. Analytics and Insights:

Provide users with insights into their productivity. Track completed tasks, time management, and goal achievement. Offer data visualization and reports.

15. Cross-Platform Compatibility:

Consider developing your app for multiple platforms, including iOS, Android, and web, to reach a broader audience. Use cross-platform development frameworks if feasible.

16. Testing and Feedback:

Thoroughly test your app to identify and fix any bugs or usability issues. Conduct usability testing with real users to gather feedback and make improvements.

17. User Support and Updates:

Offer user support channels, such as email or in-app chat, to address user inquiries and issues promptly. Regularly update your app to add new features and address user feedback.

Creating a successful productivity app requires a deep understanding of productivity workflows and user behavior. By focusing on user needs, delivering a user-friendly experience, and continuously improving your app, you can help users achieve their goals and boost their productivity.

Section 18.5: Building a Custom Launcher

Custom launchers are a unique category of Android apps that allow users to personalize the look and functionality of their device's home screen and app drawer. In this section, we'll explore the process of building a custom launcher app for Android.

1. Understanding Custom Launchers:

Custom launchers are a type of Android app that replaces the default launcher on a user's device. They provide a unique home screen experience by allowing users to customize the layout, icons, themes, and animations. Some popular custom launchers include Nova Launcher, Action Launcher, and Lawnchair.

2. Key Features of a Custom Launcher:

When building a custom launcher, consider implementing the following key features:

- **Home Screen Customization**: Allow users to customize the layout and appearance of their home screens. This includes changing the grid size, adding widgets, and arranging app icons.

- **App Drawer Customization**: Provide options for customizing the app drawer, such as sorting apps by categories, adding folders, or changing the sorting order.

- **Icon Packs**: Support icon packs that users can download and apply to change the appearance of app icons.

- **Gestures and Shortcuts**: Implement gesture controls and shortcuts for launching apps or performing actions quickly.

- **Themes and Wallpapers**: Allow users to change themes, wallpapers, and fonts to personalize the launcher's appearance.

- **Backup and Restore**: Offer backup and restore functionality to save users' customizations and settings.

3. Architecture and Components:

The architecture of a custom launcher typically consists of the following components:

- **Launcher Activity**: This is the main entry point of the launcher app. It displays the home screen and handles user interactions.

- **App Drawer**: A component that displays the list of installed apps and allows users to search for and launch them.

- **Settings**: Implement a settings screen where users can configure various aspects of the launcher, such as themes, gestures, and grid layouts.

- **Widgets**: Support widgets on the home screen, allowing users to add clock widgets, weather information, or custom widgets.

Design an intuitive and visually appealing user interface for your custom launcher. Consider offering users themes and customization options for the launcher's appearance. Ensure that the user interface elements are responsive to touch and gestures.

Custom launchers may require certain permissions, such as access to installed apps and the home screen. Ensure that you request permissions appropriately and follow Android's permission guidelines.

Thoroughly test your custom launcher on various Android devices and screen sizes to ensure compatibility. Optimize the launcher's performance to provide a smooth user experience.

When your custom launcher is ready, you can publish it on the Google Play Store or other app distribution platforms. Provide clear instructions for users on how to set your launcher as the default launcher on their devices.

Offer user support channels, such as email or in-app feedback, to address user inquiries and issues promptly. Regularly update your custom launcher to fix bugs, add new features, and improve performance based on user feedback.

Building a custom launcher is a creative endeavor that allows you to provide users with a unique and personalized Android experience. However, it's essential to ensure that your launcher is stable, responsive, and user-friendly to meet users' expectations and gain popularity in the competitive Android app market.

Chapter 19: Internationalization and Localization

In a globalized world, Android app developers need to consider a diverse audience with varying languages, cultures, and regional preferences. Internationalization (i18n) and localization (l10n) are crucial processes that enable your Android app to be used by people worldwide while providing a tailored experience for different regions. In this chapter, we'll dive into the concepts of internationalization and localization and explore how to make your Android app accessible and appealing to a global audience.

Section 19.1: Preparing Your App for Global Audiences

Before you can effectively localize your Android app, you need to ensure that it's properly internationalized. Internationalization is the process of designing your app to support multiple languages, regions, and cultures from the start. Here's what you need to consider:

1. Resource Management:

- **Strings**: Store user-visible text in resource files and use placeholders for dynamic content. Avoid hardcoding strings in your code.

- **Layouts**: Create flexible layouts that accommodate different text lengths and orientations.

2. Supporting Multiple Languages:

- **Resource Files**: Organize strings, layouts, and other resources into folders named by language and region codes (e.g., `values-en`, `values-fr-rCA`).

- **Translations**: Provide translations for all user-facing text. Android's resource system will automatically load the appropriate resources based on the user's device settings.

- **String Plurals**: Handle plural forms for languages that have different pluralization rules. Use the `plurals` resource type.

3. Formatting and Styling:

- **Date and Time**: Use Android's date and time formatting classes to display dates and times according to the user's locale.

- **Numbers**: Format numbers, currencies, and percentages based on the user's locale.

4. Right-to-Left (RTL) Support:

- Ensure that your app's layouts and text display correctly in RTL languages like Arabic and Hebrew. Android provides RTL layout support for this purpose.

5. Cultural Awareness:

- Be aware of cultural differences and sensitivities. Ensure that your app's content and imagery are culturally appropriate for the target audience.

6. Testing and Quality Assurance:

• Test your app with different language settings, including languages that use non-Latin scripts.

• Pay attention to text truncation, layout issues, and string concatenation that might not work well in some languages.

7. User Locale Settings:

• Respect the user's chosen language and region settings. Allow users to change the app's language within the app settings.

8. Third-Party Libraries and Services:

• Check if any third-party libraries or services used in your app support internationalization and localization.

By thoroughly internationalizing your Android app, you lay the foundation for successful localization. It's a proactive approach that allows you to serve a broader audience and makes the localization process more manageable. In the subsequent sections, we'll delve deeper into the localization aspect, where we'll adapt your app to specific languages, cultures, and regions.

Section 19.2: Implementing Multi-Language Support

Once you've internationalized your Android app to accommodate various languages, the next step is to localize it for specific locales or regions. This process involves translating the user-visible text, images, and other resources into different languages and adapting the app's content to suit the cultural norms of the target audience. Here's how you can effectively implement multi-language support in your Android app:

1. Resource Files for Each Language:

• Create a separate resource folder for each supported language and region. For example, you might have folders like `values-en`, `values-fr`, and `values-de` for English, French, and German translations, respectively.

• In each resource folder, include a `strings.xml` file containing translated strings. Maintain the same string resource names across all language files. For instance, if you have an English string resource called `app_name`, ensure that you have the same resource in other language files.

2. String Resource Translations:

• For each language, provide translations for all user-visible text, including labels, buttons, and messages.

• Use placeholders in your string resources to accommodate dynamic content. For example, instead of "Hello, John," use "Hello, %s" and replace `%s` with the user's name programmatically.

- Utilize the `<string-array>` resource type for string arrays that require translation.

3. Locale Detection and Selection:

- Detect the user's preferred locale and select the appropriate language and region-specific resources at runtime. Android provides APIs to help with this.

- Allow users to manually change the app's language from within the app's settings. This is especially important for users who prefer a different language than their device's default setting.

4. RTL (Right-to-Left) Languages:

- For languages that are read from right to left, such as Arabic and Hebrew, ensure that your app's layouts and text direction are adjusted accordingly.

- You can create RTL layouts and include them in the appropriate resource folders (e.g., `layout-ldrtl`) to support RTL languages.

5. Date and Time Formatting:

- Localize date and time formats based on the user's locale. Android provides the `SimpleDateFormat` class for this purpose.

- Use the appropriate date and time formatting patterns for each locale to display dates and times correctly.

6. Number and Currency Formatting:

- Format numbers, currencies, and percentages based on the user's locale. The `NumberFormat` class in Android can help you achieve this.

- Be aware of different number formats (e.g., comma as a decimal separator in some regions) and adapt your app accordingly.

7. Testing and Quality Assurance:

- Thoroughly test your app's multi-language support by changing the device's language and region settings.

- Pay attention to text truncation, layout issues, and string concatenation that might not work well in certain languages.

Implementing multi-language support in your Android app is essential for providing an inclusive and user-friendly experience to a global audience. It allows users from different linguistic backgrounds to interact with your app comfortably, increasing its accessibility and usability. In the next section, we'll explore how to handle locale and regional preferences more effectively.

Section 19.3: Handling Locale and Regional Preferences

Handling locale and regional preferences is a crucial aspect of Android app development, especially when you want to provide a personalized experience to users from different parts of the world. Android offers various tools and techniques to manage these preferences effectively. In this section, we'll explore how to handle locale and regional preferences in your Android app.

1. Locale Object:
- Android uses the Locale object to represent a user's language and regional settings. It encapsulates information such as language, country, and variant.

- You can create a Locale object based on the user's preferences and use it to format text, numbers, dates, and times accordingly.

```
Locale userLocale = new Locale("fr", "FR"); // French, France
```

2. Resource Localization:
- Android's resource system allows you to provide different resources for various locales and regions.

- To retrieve localized resources, you can use the getResources() method with the user's Locale object:

```
Resources resources = getResources();
Configuration config = resources.getConfiguration();
config.setLocale(userLocale);
resources.updateConfiguration(config, resources.getDisplayMetrics());
```

This code updates the app's configuration to use the user's selected Locale, ensuring that the appropriate resources are loaded.

3. Localized Layouts:
- In addition to string resources, you can also create layouts specific to different languages or regions.

- For example, you can have different layouts for landscape and portrait orientations or layouts optimized for right-to-left (RTL) languages.

4. Number and Currency Formatting:
- To format numbers, currencies, and percentages according to the user's locale, you can use the NumberFormat class.

- For example, to format a number as currency:

```
double amount = 1234.56;
NumberFormat currencyFormatter = NumberFormat.getCurrencyInstance(userLocale)
```

```
;
String formattedAmount = currencyFormatter.format(amount);
```

- Similarly, you can format dates and times based on the user's locale using the `SimpleDateFormat` class.

- To format a date:

```
Date now = new Date();
SimpleDateFormat dateFormatter = new SimpleDateFormat("dd MMMM yyyy", userLoc
ale);
String formattedDate = dateFormatter.format(now);
```

- For languages that are read from right to left, Android provides support for RTL layouts and text direction.

- You can create RTL layouts and specify the text direction in your XML layout files.

```
android:layoutDirection="rtl"
```

- Allow users to choose their preferred language and region within your app's settings.

- You can create a language preference screen that updates the app's `Locale` and configuration based on the user's selection.

- Thoroughly test your app with different locales and regions to ensure that text, formatting, and layouts appear correctly.

- Pay attention to the layout's alignment, text truncation, and overall usability.

Handling locale and regional preferences ensures that your Android app provides a customized experience to users from diverse linguistic and cultural backgrounds. By respecting their language and regional settings, you enhance the usability and accessibility of your app, ultimately leading to a more positive user experience. In the next section, we'll delve into best practices for effective localization.

Section 19.4: Localization Best Practices

Localization, the process of adapting your Android app for various languages and regions, is a crucial step in ensuring a global user base. In this section, we'll discuss some best practices to follow when localizing your Android app effectively.

1. Start Localization Early:

- Localization should be considered from the early stages of app development. Plan and structure your code and resources to accommodate different languages and regions.

- Use resource files for strings, layouts, and other resources to separate content from code.

2. Use String Resources:

- Always store text that appears in your app's UI in string resources. Avoid hardcoding text in your code files.

- Android's resource system allows you to provide separate string resources for different languages and regions.

```
<string name="welcome_message">Welcome!</string>
```

- Create separate `strings.xml` files for each language, such as `values-en/strings.xml` for English and `values-fr/strings.xml` for French.

3. Support Plurals and Gender:

- Different languages have different rules for plurals and gender. Android provides a way to handle these variations using the `<plurals>` and `<string>` elements in your resource files.

```
<!-- Example for pluralization -->
<plurals name="apples">
    <item quantity="one">One apple</item>
    <item quantity="other">%d apples</item>
</plurals>
```

4. Localize Images and Layouts:

- Images with text should also be localized. Use different images or overlay text on images based on the language.

- For layouts, consider differences in text length. Languages like German often have longer words, which may affect the layout.

5. Test on Real Devices:

- Test your app on real devices with different screen sizes and resolutions. Ensure that text and UI elements adapt correctly.

6. Use Contextual Information:

- Understand the cultural context of your target audience. Translate and adapt content accordingly.

- Be mindful of cultural references, idioms, and humor that may not translate well.

- Support languages that read from right to left (e.g., Arabic and Hebrew) by creating layouts and text direction settings for right-to-left (RTL) languages.

8. Handle Date and Time Formats:

- Use Android's date and time formatting classes to display dates and times in a way that is familiar to users in different regions.

- Respect date and time format preferences set in the user's device settings.

9. User-Selectable Language:

- Provide a language selection option within your app's settings. Allow users to override the device's default language.

- Ensure that the selected language persists across app sessions.

10. Localize App Store Listing:

- Localize your app's title, description, and screenshots on the app store. This helps users discover your app in their preferred language.

11. Collaborate with Native Speakers:

- If possible, collaborate with native speakers or professional translators who are familiar with the language and culture.

- Use translation management tools to streamline the localization process.

12. Regular Updates:

- Continue to update and improve your localized content based on user feedback and changes in the app.

Effective localization can significantly enhance your app's user experience and broaden its reach. By considering these best practices, you can create an inclusive and accessible app for users around the world. In the next section, we'll explore how to test internationalization to ensure a seamless experience across languages and regions.

Section 19.5: Testing Internationalization

Testing internationalization (i18n) is a critical step in ensuring that your Android app provides a seamless experience for users in different languages and regions. In this section, we'll discuss various aspects of testing i18n to identify and resolve issues related to localization.

1. Language and Region Testing:

- Start by testing your app in different languages and regions. Switch your device's language settings to the target language and region to verify that your app's translations and localized content are displayed correctly.

- Check for issues such as text truncation, overlapping UI elements, and incorrect translations.

2. Pluralization and Gender Testing:
- Verify that your app correctly handles plural forms and gender-specific content. Use languages with different pluralization rules and gender requirements to test this functionality.

- Check if the correct plural forms and gender-specific translations are displayed based on the quantity and gender of the content.

3. BiDi (Right-to-Left) Language Testing:
- Test your app's support for right-to-left (BiDi) languages like Arabic and Hebrew. Ensure that UI elements, text alignment, and layout adapt properly when using BiDi languages.

- Verify that the app's UI remains functional and visually appealing in BiDi mode.

4. Date and Time Format Testing:
- Test date and time formatting in your app by setting your device to different regions. Ensure that dates and times are displayed correctly based on the user's locale.

- Verify that the app respects the date and time format preferences set in the device's settings.

5. User-Selectable Language Testing:
- Test the language selection feature within your app. Check if the selected language persists across app sessions and if the app's content updates accordingly.

- Verify that the app maintains the selected language even when the device's system language changes.

6. Localization Testing on Different Devices:
- Test your app on various Android devices with different screen sizes, resolutions, and aspect ratios. Ensure that the UI elements adapt correctly to different screen configurations.

- Check for layout issues, such as text truncation or overlapping elements, on devices with smaller or larger screens.

7. Accessibility Testing:
- Conduct accessibility testing to ensure that your app remains usable for users with disabilities in different languages and regions.

- Test screen readers, voice commands, and other accessibility features with localized content.

8. Edge Cases and Special Characters:

- Test edge cases, such as languages with complex scripts or languages that use special characters. Ensure that these languages are supported without issues.

- Verify that input fields and text handling functions correctly with special characters.

9. Local Data Testing:

- Test how your app handles local data, such as currency symbols, number formats, and units of measurement. Check that these elements are displayed correctly based on the user's locale.

- Verify that calculations and conversions involving local data are accurate.

10. User Feedback and Beta Testing:

- Encourage users from different regions to provide feedback on the localized versions of your app. Beta testing with a diverse group of users can help uncover issues that may not be apparent during development.

- Act on user feedback to make necessary improvements to the app's localization.

11. Regression Testing:

- Perform regression testing after making updates or changes to your app's localization. Ensure that new changes do not introduce issues in previously working localized versions.

By thoroughly testing internationalization, you can deliver a high-quality app experience to users around the world. Regular testing and continuous improvement are essential to maintain the integrity of your app's localization as it evolves over time. In the next chapter, we'll explore the future of Android development and emerging technologies in the Android ecosystem.

Chapter 20: The Future of Android Development

Section 20.1: Emerging Android Technologies

The world of Android development is continually evolving, driven by technological advancements and changing user demands. In this section, we'll explore some emerging Android technologies and trends that are shaping the future of app development.

1. Foldable and Dual-Screen Devices:
- With the introduction of foldable and dual-screen Android devices, developers have new opportunities to create innovative user experiences. These devices provide extra screen real estate and unique interaction possibilities.

- Developers can adapt their apps to take advantage of these larger displays and create seamless transitions between folded and unfolded modes.

2. 5G Connectivity:
- The rollout of 5G networks is revolutionizing mobile connectivity. It enables faster data speeds, lower latency, and the potential for entirely new types of apps and services.

- Developers can explore opportunities in augmented reality (AR), virtual reality (VR), real-time gaming, and multimedia streaming that benefit from high-speed, low-latency 5G connections.

3. Machine Learning and AI:
- Machine learning and artificial intelligence are increasingly integrated into Android apps. Developers can leverage ML frameworks like TensorFlow Lite and ML Kit to create apps that offer personalized experiences, object recognition, and more.

- AI-driven features, such as chatbots and predictive analytics, can enhance user engagement and efficiency.

4. Augmented Reality (AR):
- AR experiences are becoming more accessible on Android devices. Google's ARCore and ARKit for Android and iOS, respectively, make it easier for developers to create AR apps.

- Industries like gaming, retail, education, and healthcare are exploring AR for immersive and interactive experiences.

5. Internet of Things (IoT):
- Android Things, Google's IoT platform, allows developers to build applications for smart devices. IoT integration extends the capabilities of Android apps to control and monitor IoT devices.

- Home automation, wearable technology, and smart city initiatives present opportunities for Android developers to innovate.

6. Jetpack Compose:
- Jetpack Compose is a modern, declarative UI toolkit for building native Android UIs. It simplifies UI development by using a composable and reactive approach.

- Developers can expect increased productivity and more maintainable code when adopting Jetpack Compose for UI development.

7. Kotlin as the Preferred Language:
- Kotlin has gained significant traction as the preferred programming language for Android app development. Google officially endorsed Kotlin in 2017, and its concise syntax and powerful features have made it a favorite among developers.

- As Kotlin continues to evolve, developers can benefit from its modern language features and enhanced tooling.

8. Instant Apps:
- Instant Apps allow users to try out Android apps without installation. This technology streamlines user acquisition and engagement.

- Developers can create instant experiences that load quickly and provide core functionality, encouraging users to install the full app.

9. App Bundles and Dynamic Delivery:
- Android App Bundles simplify app distribution by providing a more efficient way to package and deliver apps. Dynamic Delivery ensures that users download only the components they need for their specific device.

- This technology optimizes app size, reduces installation time, and improves user retention.

10. Privacy and Security:
- As user privacy concerns grow, Android development places a strong emphasis on data protection and security. Developers need to stay informed about best practices, secure coding, and compliance with privacy regulations.

- Features like Scoped Storage and runtime permissions enhance user data security.

These emerging technologies and trends represent exciting opportunities for Android developers to create innovative and impactful apps. Staying updated and experimenting with these technologies will be essential to succeed in the dynamic world of Android app development. In the next section, we'll discuss current and future trends in app development that developers should watch out for.

Section 20.2: Trends in App Development

The field of mobile app development is constantly evolving, driven by technological advancements and changing user expectations. In this section, we'll explore some prominent trends in app development that are shaping the industry.

1. Cross-Platform Development:

- Cross-platform development frameworks like Flutter, React Native, and Xamarin are gaining popularity. They allow developers to write code once and deploy it on multiple platforms, reducing development time and effort.

- These frameworks provide native-like performance and access to device features, making them attractive options for building apps for both Android and iOS.

2. Progressive Web Apps (PWAs):

- PWAs are web applications that offer a native app-like experience within a web browser. They are fast, reliable, and provide offline capabilities through service workers.

- Developers are increasingly adopting PWAs to reach a broader audience, as they can run on various platforms and do not require app store installations.

3. Artificial Intelligence (AI) and Machine Learning (ML):

- AI and ML technologies are being integrated into apps to provide personalized user experiences, predictive analytics, and automation.

- Chatbots, recommendation engines, and image recognition are just a few examples of AI-driven features that enhance user engagement.

4. Internet of Things (IoT) Integration:

- The IoT ecosystem is expanding, and developers are creating apps that can control and monitor smart devices. This trend is particularly relevant in home automation, healthcare, and industrial applications.

- IoT integration offers users greater convenience and control over their connected devices.

5. Blockchain Technology:

- Blockchain is finding its way into various industries, including finance, supply chain, and healthcare. App developers are exploring blockchain for secure and transparent data management.

- Blockchain can enable features like secure transactions, provenance tracking, and digital identity verification within apps.

6. Voice User Interfaces (VUI):

- With the growing popularity of smart speakers and voice assistants, VUI is becoming a significant trend. Developers are creating voice-enabled apps that allow users to interact with technology using natural language.

- Integrating voice recognition and synthesis into apps enhances accessibility and convenience.

7. Augmented Reality (AR) and Virtual Reality (VR):

- AR and VR technologies continue to evolve, offering immersive experiences. Apps in gaming, education, training, and retail are integrating AR and VR to engage users in new ways.

- The introduction of ARKit and ARCore has made AR more accessible to mobile app developers.

8. Enhanced Security and Privacy:

- App security and user data privacy are paramount. Developers are implementing robust security measures, such as encryption, secure authentication, and data protection.

- Compliance with regulations like GDPR and CCPA is essential for apps that handle user data.

9. Serverless Computing:

- Serverless architectures, using platforms like AWS Lambda and Google Cloud Functions, are simplifying backend development. Developers can focus on writing code without managing servers.

- Serverless computing reduces infrastructure costs and improves scalability.

10. Low-Code/No-Code Development:

- Low-code and no-code platforms empower users with limited coding experience to build functional apps quickly.

- These platforms enable rapid prototyping and collaboration between developers and non-technical stakeholders.

Staying informed about these trends and adopting relevant technologies can help app developers remain competitive and deliver outstanding user experiences. Embracing innovation and adaptability is key to success in the dynamic landscape of app development.

Section 20.3: Preparing for Android Updates

Android, as an operating system, continually evolves with updates and new versions. These updates introduce enhancements, bug fixes, security patches, and new features. In this section, we'll explore the importance of preparing for Android updates as an app developer.

1. Stay Informed:
- Keeping abreast of Android's release schedule and updates is vital. Google typically releases a major Android version annually, with security patches and maintenance updates in between.

- Google's Android Developers website, blogs, and official announcements are excellent sources for staying informed about updates.

2. Test on Beta Versions:
- Google often provides beta versions of upcoming Android updates. Participating in beta testing allows you to ensure your app is compatible with new features and changes.

- Beta testing helps identify and fix issues before the official release, improving user experience.

3. Update SDKs and Libraries:
- Regularly update your app's SDKs, libraries, and dependencies to their latest versions. Library updates may include optimizations and fixes for compatibility with new Android versions.

- Ensure that any deprecated APIs or features are replaced with their recommended alternatives.

4. Target Latest API Levels:
- Google encourages developers to target the latest Android API levels. Doing so ensures that your app can take advantage of new features and optimizations while remaining compatible with older devices.

- However, remember to set appropriate minimum API levels to maintain compatibility with a broad user base.

5. Adopt New Features:
- Embrace new Android features that enhance your app's functionality and user experience. Features like Dark Mode, gesture navigation, and biometric authentication can improve user satisfaction.

- Make sure to communicate these updates to your users through release notes and documentation.

6. Optimize for Performance:
- Android updates often bring performance improvements and optimizations. Use profiling tools to identify bottlenecks and areas for performance enhancement.

- App performance impacts user retention and ratings, so optimizing your app for new Android versions is crucial.

7. Ensure Compatibility:

- Thoroughly test your app on various devices running different Android versions. Ensure that it functions correctly, displays well on different screen sizes, and handles any platform-specific changes.

- Address compatibility issues promptly to prevent negative user feedback.

8. Consider Privacy and Security:

- Android updates may introduce changes to privacy and security requirements. Stay informed about these changes and ensure your app complies with the latest guidelines.

- Regularly review and update your app's privacy policy and security measures.

9. Backward Compatibility:

- While targeting the latest Android version is essential, maintaining backward compatibility is equally important. Many users may not immediately upgrade their devices.

- Implement feature flags and conditionally adapt your app's behavior for different Android versions.

10. User Communication:

- Keep your users informed about how your app benefits from Android updates. Mention any new features, performance improvements, and security enhancements in your release notes.

- Maintain an active support channel to address user queries and issues related to updates.

By proactively preparing for Android updates, you can ensure that your app remains relevant, functional, and secure across different Android versions. This approach not only enhances the user experience but also demonstrates your commitment to providing a top-quality app.

Section 20.4: Community and Resources

In the world of Android development, being part of a community and accessing valuable resources can significantly impact your growth and success. This section explores the importance of community involvement and provides insights into the resources available to Android developers.

1. Join Android Developer Communities:

- Android has a vibrant developer community. Participate in forums, discussion boards, and social media groups where developers exchange ideas, solve problems, and share knowledge.

- Communities like Stack Overflow, Reddit's r/androiddev, and Google's official Android Developers community are great places to connect with peers.

2. Attend Meetups and Conferences:
- Local Android developer meetups and conferences offer excellent opportunities for networking and learning. They often feature talks by industry experts and provide insights into the latest trends and technologies.

- Keep an eye out for events like DroidCon, Android Dev Summit, and local developer gatherings.

3. Follow Influential Developers:
- Identify influential Android developers and follow them on social media platforms like Twitter, LinkedIn, and GitHub. They often share valuable insights, code samples, and updates.

- Engaging with these developers can lead to meaningful collaborations and knowledge exchange.

4. Explore Open Source Projects:
- Contributing to open source Android projects is an excellent way to enhance your skills and give back to the community. Platforms like GitHub host numerous Android-related repositories.

- You can learn from existing codebases, fix bugs, and collaborate with other developers.

5. Read Android Blogs and Tutorials:
- Many experienced Android developers maintain blogs and publish tutorials. These resources can help you learn new concepts and stay up-to-date with best practices.

- Subscribe to blogs like Android Developers Blog, Medium publications, and independent Android developer blogs.

6. Android Documentation:
- Google's official Android Developer website provides comprehensive documentation. It's an essential resource for understanding Android APIs, guidelines, and best practices.

- Always refer to official documentation when working on Android projects.

7. Online Courses and Learning Platforms:
- Platforms like Udacity, Udemy, and Coursera offer Android development courses. These courses are suitable for both beginners and experienced developers looking to expand their skills.

- Explore courses on topics like Kotlin, Android Jetpack, and app architecture.

8. YouTube Tutorials:
- YouTube hosts a wealth of Android development tutorials. Many experienced developers create video content to explain various topics visually.

- Videos can be a great way to learn about Android development techniques.

9. GitHub Repositories:
- GitHub is a treasure trove of Android projects and code samples. You can find everything from complete apps to libraries and utilities.

- Explore repositories related to your areas of interest.

10. Android Developer Tools:
- Familiarize yourself with essential developer tools like Android Studio, Android Emulator, and the Android Debug Bridge (ADB).

- Learning to use these tools effectively can significantly boost your productivity.

By actively engaging with the Android development community and leveraging available resources, you can continuously improve your skills, stay updated with industry trends, and create high-quality Android apps. Remember that learning and growth in the field are ongoing processes, and community involvement plays a vital role in your journey as an Android developer.

Section 20.5: Career Paths in Android Development

Android development offers a diverse range of career paths, making it an exciting field for aspiring developers. In this section, we will explore various career options and considerations for those pursuing a career in Android development.

1. Android App Developer:
- The most common career path for Android developers is becoming an app developer. App developers create, design, and maintain Android applications for various purposes, from gaming to productivity.

- This role requires a strong understanding of Java or Kotlin, Android SDK, and user interface design.

2. UI/UX Designer:
- UI/UX (User Interface/User Experience) designers focus on creating visually appealing and user-friendly app interfaces. They work closely with developers to ensure that apps are intuitive and visually engaging.

- A combination of design skills and understanding of Android's UI components is crucial in this role.

3. Mobile Software Engineer:

- Mobile software engineers specialize in building mobile software solutions, not limited to Android alone. They may work on cross-platform development using technologies like Flutter or React Native.

- This role requires knowledge of multiple mobile platforms and frameworks.

4. Android Game Developer:

- Game development on Android is a specialized field. Game developers create interactive and engaging games for mobile devices, utilizing game engines like Unity or Unreal Engine.

- Proficiency in game development, physics, and graphics programming is essential.

5. Android Framework Developer:

- Framework developers work on Android's core libraries and system components. They contribute to the Android Open Source Project (AOSP) and help shape the Android platform itself.

- This role demands a deep understanding of Android's internals and C/C++ programming skills.

6. Android Freelancer:

- Freelancers have the flexibility to work on various Android projects for different clients. They often have a broad skill set and adapt to different project requirements.

- Freelancing allows for a diverse range of experiences but requires strong project management and client communication skills.

7. Android Instructor or Trainer:

- Experienced Android developers can transition into teaching roles, either through online courses, tutorials, or in-person training.

- Effective communication and the ability to simplify complex concepts are crucial for this role.

8. Android Product Manager:

- Product managers oversee the development and lifecycle of Android apps. They bridge the gap between development teams, stakeholders, and users to ensure the success of the product.

- This role involves project management, market analysis, and strategic planning.

9. Android QA Tester:

- Quality Assurance testers ensure the functionality and performance of Android apps by conducting rigorous testing and reporting issues.

- Attention to detail and the ability to identify and reproduce bugs are vital skills.

10. Android Security Analyst:

- Security analysts specialize in identifying and mitigating security vulnerabilities in Android applications. They play a critical role in protecting user data.

- This role requires knowledge of security best practices and penetration testing.

11. Android DevOps Engineer:

- DevOps engineers focus on automating app deployment, testing, and infrastructure management. They ensure smooth and efficient app delivery pipelines.

- Proficiency in tools like Jenkins, Docker, and continuous integration is key.

When considering your Android development career path, it's essential to align your interests, skills, and goals. Additionally, the Android ecosystem is dynamic, so staying updated with emerging technologies and trends is crucial for career growth. Whether you choose to specialize in app development, UI/UX design, or another role, Android offers a multitude of opportunities for those passionate about mobile technology.

www.ingramcontent.com/pod-product-compliance
Lightning Source LLC
Chambersburg PA
CBHW052150070326
40690CB00048B/2212